DATA PRIVACY –

PRACTICAL HANDBOOK FOR GOVERNANCE & OPERATIONS

MUNEEB IMRAN SHAIKH

TAHIR LATIF

TABLE OF CONTENTS

DEDICATIONS

To my parents and my brothers, who have been kind to me and supported me.

To my wife and children (Zeeniya & Aliyar), who have always supported me in my pursuits through their patience, love, understanding, and all the unwavering support and sacrifices they rendered to enable me to put in long hours for writing this book.

To Imran Khan (Pakistan's Cricket Team Captain and Philanthropist) and two mentors in my personal life who taught me the significance of perseverance, determination, and the ability to rise above one's own benefits and contribute to the overall well-being of society.

Muneeb Imran Shaikh

To my beloved family, whose unwavering love, patience, and support have been my constant anchor and my greatest source of strength.

To every privacy professional tirelessly striving to protect the dignity and rights of individuals in an increasingly complex digital world.

Tahir Latif

ACKNOWLEDGMENTS

We sincerely believe that our book would not have been possible without the significant contributions, support, and encouragement of various individuals involved in our journey.

We would like to begin by thanking our peers, industry experts, and our professional mentors in the field of personal data protection. We would also like to thank the following peers working in information security, governance, and risk management sectors. We thank them for sharpening and refining our perspectives, challenging our fundamental assumptions, and providing valuable support throughout our journey.

We wish to express special gratitude to our colleagues who shared real-world insights, case studies that helped to bring more nuance to the discourse in this book.

We extend deepest appreciation to the editorial team and reviewers whose diligence and attention to detail ensured clarity, accuracy, structure, and coherence.

Lastly, we want to thank all those privacy professionals, data ethicists, and regulatory bodies that are working to uphold and protect the bastion of human dignity and autonomy. Your work carries enormous strength and value to human societies.

Muneeb Imran Shaikh

No book is ever the work of one person alone. This work owes its existence to the guidance, collaboration, and encouragement of many extraordinary people and organizations who have shaped and supported it along the way.

I am deeply grateful to my family and to my co-author Muneeb, who stood by me through long nights of research and countless revisions, offering both solace and inspiration. Your unwavering belief in this project sustained me.

My heartfelt appreciation goes to Azher Malik, Joyce Varkey, and Basmah Alsubaie for their steadfast support, insightful conversations, and invaluable encouragement throughout my privacy journey.

To my colleagues and mentors in the privacy, AI governance, and regulatory communities, thank you for challenging my thinking, expanding my perspective, and generously sharing your expertise.

I am especially thankful to the global experts and practitioners who candidly discussed real-world challenges with me. Your openness has enriched the practical insights reflected in this book.

And to my clients around the world—thank you for placing your trust in me. Guiding your data privacy and AI journeys has been both an honor and a driving force behind my continued passion to push boundaries and innovate.

Tahir Latif

ABOUT THE AUTHORS

Tahir is a globally recognised data privacy expert and a leading advisor on responsible and ethical AI. Known for his charismatic, methodical, and client-focused approach, he has guided global organisations through complex privacy and AI governance challenges. As Chief Privacy and AI Governance Officer, he has led groundbreaking work on global data protection strategies, cross-border compliance, and operationalising responsible AI frameworks.

He is a trusted advisor to governments, regulators, and C-suite leaders, providing strategic guidance on data privacy, AI governance, and regulatory alignment. He is also an active participant in international panels, a keynote speaker at major industry events, and a contributor to thought leadership initiatives, including training programs for the next generation of AI governance professionals.

Muneeb Imran Shaikh is an established and credible voice in the field of Data Privacy, AI Governance, and Information Security.

His work spans AI governance and ethics, privacy program development, cybersecurity strategy, and regulatory compliance across complex Information Security and Privacy frameworks.

Muneeb has worked with entities in finance, telecom, and government sectors, building programs that reflect both legal obligations and emerging risk landscapes.

Muneeb's influence extends beyond strategy development and execution. He actively contributes to the global privacy and security discourse through long-form writing, podcast appearances, and in-depth policy reviews. He speaks at regional and international forums on topics ranging from responsible AI to privacy governance and adherence to regulations.

His work is known for translating complex governance challenges into practical insights that resonate with practitioners, regulators, and business leaders alike.

PREFACE

Privacy as a concept has remained common across all religions, cultures, and ideologies. Therefore, we believe that data privacy cannot afford to be an abstract concept, nor should it be discussed solely in the language of compliance and regulations.

Privacy is fundamental to ensure human dignity and autonomy. It may be surprising for some of the Data Privacy experts or professionals to find out that the understanding of privacy is varied and, at times, significantly lower than in many sections of societies regardless of the socio-economic background, culture, religion or other social structures through which we define ourselves.

In addition, those who do understand this subject and are working to implement the Data Privacy function within the organizations often remain occupied with the thought of fulfilling the regulatory requirements without paying enough attention to the values that need to be upheld by the very articles of the Personal Data Protection laws.

Without a firm grasp on the moral and ethical underpinnings any attempt to build systems, policies, or laws around privacy may not yield desired outcomes.

This book is, therefore, written to build a requisite understanding of privacy. Reading it will help us to understand how our rights are linked to data in the modern world. Once the privacy of individuals is compromised, it opens the floodgates for our other rights as individuals to be compromised or denied.

We begin by examining the philosophical and social aspects of privacy, inviting readers to reflect on why it matters in both personal and societal contexts. We then explore the governance mechanisms needed to translate privacy principles into accountable systems, and we discuss the structures that uphold the spirit of the law, not just its written provisions. Finally, we turn to operational realities, offering practical insights for implementing privacy in a way that is sustainable, contextually relevant, and responsive to evolving risks. We have made a conscious choice not to club the various topics in the form of chapters, and instead broken them down into three major sections, with the aim to help our readers take a crisp view of the subject.

By delving into the specific examples discussed within the book, we intend to sensitize the readers, regardless of their professional or socio-economic backgrounds, about the data that defines us and how our autonomy, dignity, rights, and liberty of choice are linked to the personal data. Through this book, we also intend to exhort data privacy professionals to see privacy beyond the lens of the compliance and regulation because if the privacy regulations and organizational privacy governance and operating model fails to uphold the rights, freedoms and interests of the individuals then it loses its purpose of existence and in fact becomes a tool to eye-wash all unethical practices around data.

This book is a guide for those who want to lead with determination and commitment. It is particularly valuable for those who have a background or are working as data protection officers, governance professionals, policymakers, and technologists who understand that privacy is not just about data. It is about people. In short, our goal is to empower readers with both the conceptual clarity and practical tools to make privacy real and necessary in this digital world.

FOREWORD

Lori Baker – Vice President – Data Protection Authority

(Middle East, African & South Asian Region)

In an era where data privacy discourse has become increasingly dominated by checkbox exercises and regulatory tick-lists, this work dares to ask the fundamental question that too many of us lose sight of: Who does privacy matter to the most and why?

Having collaborated across the ups and downs of data protection law for several years, I have witnessed firsthand Tahir's and Muneeb's unwavering commitment to viewing privacy not as a compliance burden, but as a cornerstone of human dignity. This perspective, eloquently articulated in this work, emerges from deep practical experience combined with philosophical reflection, which is a rare combination in our field.

The central thesis—that privacy cannot be divorced from its moral and ethical foundations— arrives at a critical juncture. As societies become increasingly "datafied", we face the very real prospect that our thoughts, preferences, and behavioral patterns will be codified, analyzed, and potentially weaponized against us. The hypothetical scenarios presented in this book are not science fiction; they are logical extensions of current technological capabilities and regulatory frameworks.

What sets this work apart is its refusal to accept the false dichotomy between technological progress and individual rights. The authors demonstrate that robust privacy protections are not obstacles to innovation but essential guardrails that ensure technological advancement serves human flourishing rather than undermining it. This is particularly evident in the discussion of how shifts in personal preferences could be interpreted rightly or wrongly by AI and other autonomous systems.

The book's treatment of the "datafication of societies" is both sobering and inspiring. The authors persuade us to confront an uncomfortable truth: in our rush to embrace a data-driven world and economy, we have often failed to consider the human cost. The result is not just a loss of privacy, but a pervasive and growing threat to human autonomy and dignity.

As someone who has spent countless hours crafting privacy notices and conducting data protection impact assessments, I found the authors' perspective of our profession particularly valuable. The observation that "data privacy professionals assume that privacy notices are adequate to ensure transparency" cuts to the heart of a systemic problem, which is one of many. We have become so focused on the mechanics of compliance that we have lost sight of its purpose: protecting real people from real harms.

In addition, this book calls on technologists to consider not just what they can build, but what they should build. As artificial intelligence systems become more sophisticated and pervasive, the need for privacy frameworks rooted in human rights principles becomes ever more urgent. The authors' vision of privacy as "a valve in society to prevent unfair outcomes" provides a compelling alternative to taking on these challenges.

I recommend this work not only to my fellow data protection practitioners, but to anyone who cares about the kind of society we are building in the digital age. The authors have given us more than a treatise on privacy law; they have provided a manifesto for human dignity in an age of algorithms.

Read this book. Share it. Most importantly, it answers the question above about the relationship between data, technology, and human rights: privacy matters the most to each one of us, because those incredibly valuable data characteristics make us who and what we are.

EXPERT REVIEWS

"This work is a valuable addition to the literature on data protection, combining rigorous legal analysis with a critical reading of contemporary digital challenges. The book reflects a deep awareness of the urgent need to develop human-centric legislative frameworks that safeguard dignity and individual rights in the face of expanding data collection and processing practices."

H.E. Dr Tariq A. Alsheddi Ex-President, National Data Management Office (NDMO)

Kingdom of Saudi Arabia

"This book brilliantly addresses a critical issue facing an AI-obsessed world: data privacy. There are few who possess Tahir and Muneeb's knowledge and experience who could write so authoritatively on this subject. An excellent exposition of an important topic."

Professor Evan Shellshear, University of Queensland.

Co-author of the bestselling book: "Why Data Science Projects Fail".

"A masterful and deeply insightful guide, this book reframes privacy not as a technical challenge, but as a profoundly human endeavour. Essential reading for data protection officers, governance professionals, policymakers, and technologists, it provides the conceptual clarity and pragmatic tools needed to champion privacy in today's digital landscape. An empowering resource for anyone determined to make privacy real and necessary."

Basmah Alsubaie - CEO of Privacy Professionals

"Muneeb and Tahir have done an excellent job by highlighting the need for data privacy clauses in modern law. Using hypotheses in this data-centric world is a great way of advocacy."

Immaculate Kassait, MBS, Data Protection Commissioner – Kenya

"This book is an essential read for any privacy professional looking to move beyond compliance and seeking to uphold the spirit of data protection. Written by well-known and respected leaders in Privacy and Responsible AI, it goes beyond the regulations to explore the moral and ethical

foundations of privacy, giving practical guidance to integrate privacy at the deepest levels of an organisation."

-Stuart Melville Data Protection Officer.

"The authors, Tahir and Muneeb, unpacked key concepts and points that immensely contribute to the development of the much-needed literature on the subject matter."

Tsitsi Mariwo - Director of Data Protection, Postal and Telecommunications Regulatory Authority – Zimbabwe.

"The authors simplify data protection, providing privacy professionals with the essential skills to succeed, including legal expertise, technical know-how, and practical guidance. A vital resource for anyone managing challenging privacy issues"

Federico Marengo PhD Assoc. Partner - White Label Consultancy

"Tahir is a global leader in data privacy and brings both depth and clarity to complex issues. This book demonstrates that privacy is not just about regulations, but also about values, fairness, and how data impacts societies. This book is of real value to privacy practitioners, enthusiasts, and also policy makers."

-Mehboob Uddin Ahmed

DPO - Qatar National Bank

SECTION I
PHILOSOPHY BEHIND
PRIVACY

1. INTRODUCTION TO DATA PRIVACY

Humans have an innate nature to codify their experiences. We codify our experiences in the form of memories within our memory banks to ensure that we can reconnect with them, identify them, and also to cherish them.

This ability not only enables us to establish neural pathways within our memory banks but also to establish connections and communication links with others. For example, think about how we name shapes like "box," "cylinder," or "circle." By using common labels, we make it easier to share ideas and understand each other. The mere act of defining or coding the object in our brains helps us to create a connection with our fellow human beings about a particular discourse underway.

It is this pursuit of our desire to codify everything that has led to the datafication of societies. In this regard, data becomes a medium that enables the codification of our identities and experiences, and then it can be further pruned to generate intelligence from it for the overall benefit of society.

While the pursuit of codification has led to increased datafication of the society, the desire for individual privacy has remained consistent across centuries.

Because of this, the European Council of Human Rights and the Universal Declaration of Human Rights consider the Right to Privacy as a fundamental human value.

However, Privacy is not a concept that has emerged in recent centuries. It has been a concept that has always found its significance and relevance in all sections of societies and cultures regardless of religions, cultures, and ethnicities.

There are various provisions in the Universal Declaration of Human Rights to safeguard the privacy and dignity of human beings.

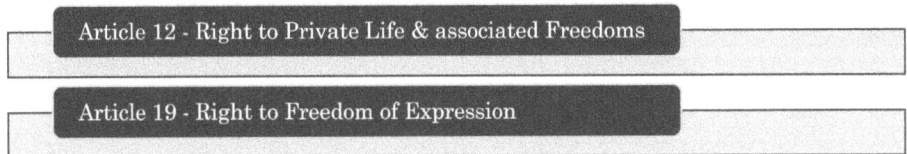

> Article 12 - Right to Private Life & associated Freedoms

> Article 19 - Right to Freedom of Expression

Figure 1 - Human Rights Declaration Articles

These articles attempt to codify the principles that were later enshrined in various data privacy laws and regulations. It can be stated that Privacy acts as a **valve** in society to prevent unfair outcomes that individuals can suffer because of breaches in their private lives and related matters.

1.1 Datafication of Societies

Human societies have historically relied on information and data to innovate and create value within society. Businesses, Medical facility providers, and government entities have always relied on information and data to deliver services, create products and contribute towards the overall socio-economic growth of society. However, the size, structure, and usability of the data have varied throughout human history.

Today data has become a commodity to be readily exchanged between different organizational entities to offer various products and services either within the countries or outside a specific country.

Moreover, better computational capabilities have enabled businesses and public and private organizations to better structure their data in the form of huge databases and run analytics over it to generate business intelligence and contribute towards the value creation.

With these computational and analytical capabilities, there are increasing avenues to develop profiles of human behaviour around their purchasing habits, genetic profiling, their travel history, medical history etc. While these capabilities add value to human society, they also come with risks of intruding into the privacy of individuals within the society.

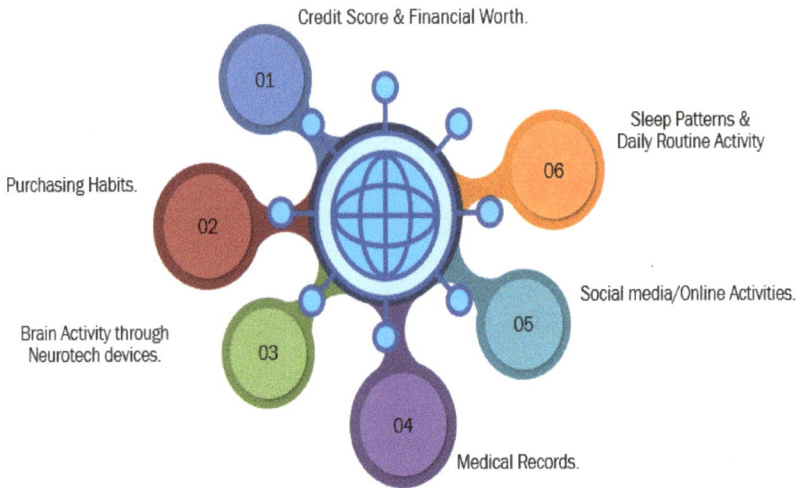

Figure 2 - Examples of Datafication in Societies

1.2 What Constitutes Personal Data?

Any data that can be used to identify an individual, whether directly or indirectly, is considered personal data. The direct identifier is the information that is specific to the individual and distinguishes one individual from another, while the indirect identifiers can be shared across a group of individuals.

Direct Identifiers	Indirect Identifiers
1. Name. 2. National ID. 3. Passport Information. 4. Social Security Numbers. 5. Medical and Health Records. 6. Genetic Information.	1. Eating and Living Habits. 2. Personal Preferences. 3. Gender. 4. Race & Ethnicity 5. Religion. 6. Political and Social Affiliations. 7. Address or Location

The above provided examples are non-exhaustive in nature. But it attempts to shed light on the discrete data sets that can negatively impact the privacy of the individual once combined.

4

Consider a person belonging to a specific race and gender applies for a job, and the Human Resources collects the racial or ethnic information to decide about the appropriateness of the candidate for the vacancy.

This exchange of Sensitive Personal data heightens the risk of harm to the individual largely due to biased or prejudiced decision-making.

Consider the example of genetic data that unearths details about medical conditions and the potential risks for the occurrence of diseases. The utility of genetic data is very high in the field of medical science. Still, In general terms of genetics, it can provide information about individuals' hereditary and ancestral lineage and traits. By having exposure to the genetic data for a single person in a family, similar lineage or ancestral traits can be identified and determined for the other family members.

1.3 Data Protection Principles

With the emergence of Data Privacy laws, regulations, and standards, we have witnessed that each instrument attempts to lay forward the core principles to be upheld. All these principles carry convergences among them since these are based on international and converged wisdom. ISO 29100 Privacy Framework laid out their 11 privacy principles within the framework, which are worth understanding and the underlying essence behind those principles. These principles are knitted together to establish an equilibrium around ensuring personal data protection and safeguarding individuals/data subject rights.

The underlying theme across all these laws, regulations and frameworks is to ensure that the asymmetric information and power between the entities processing personal data and the individuals whose personal data is being processed is reduced.

As we examine each of these principles, we will learn how each of these principles plays a significant role in restoring the symmetry of information and power through various regulations.

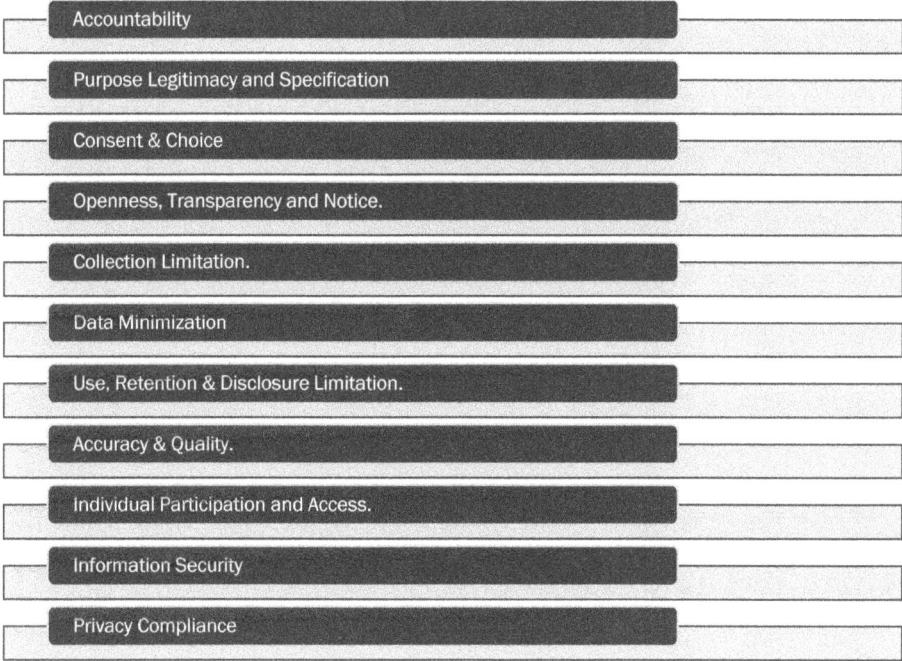

Figure 3 - ISO 29100 Privacy Principles.

1. ACCOUNTABILITY

Personal data acts as a fuel to run business operations where the business revenue streams are heavily dependent on the collection and processing of personal data. The ability to collect and/or process personal data shifts the information and power balance in favour of the organizations when compared to the individuals. It is, therefore, critical that the organization is held accountable for all the personal data that is available at its disposal.

The idea behind the accountability principle is to maintain the equilibrium between the organizations and individuals whose personal data is being processed. However, the principle of accountability is not established only by virtue of the functional unit bearing the responsibility of daily data privacy tasks.

To ensure the principle of accountability is deeply rooted within the organization, it is imperative to have appropriate policies, procedures, and frameworks along with an effective

6

operating model to govern and provide oversight to data privacy functions and their various underlying aspects and procedures.

By having approved policies, procedures and frameworks overseen by respective management and board committees, organizations can ensure that accountability checks are placed at various levels of the organization so that the other principles of personal data processing are consistently adhered to.

In the same manner, the underlying objectives desired with accountability principles cannot be attained if other principles are ignored or if they are poorly implemented.

2. PURPOSE LEGITIMACY AND SPECIFICATION

The personal data collected and processed by the organizations must have a legal basis behind it. It means that the organizations must be able to explain to the individuals the legal reason for them to process such personal data.

There are several legal grounds for processing personal data, which are often outlined in the relevant laws and regulations. EU- GDPR Article 6 identifies six legal grounds for processing, which are shown in the figure below.

The principle of Purpose legitimacy and specification attempts to ensure that organizations will not leverage their computation and processing powers to their benefit and without any regard for the individuals' interest. It requires the organizations to be able to identify and justify the nature of personal data processing being undertaken within the organization.

It also requires that the organizations shall collect and process personal data in accordance with the principles of Limit data collection after a legal ground has been established.

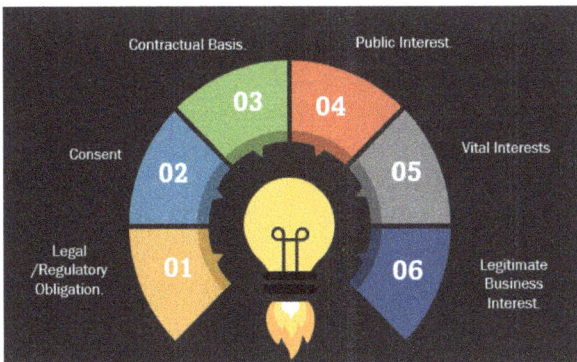

Figure 4 - Lawfulness of Personal Data Processing in EU GDPR - Article 6

3. CONSENT & CHOICE

Consent and Choice are central to restoring the asymmetrical relationships between the organizations, and the individuals where the individuals are provided the choice and the consent is sought against the collection or processing of personal data.

Consent is a very powerful and legal expression afforded to the individuals that empowers the individuals to decide what kind of personal data processing can be permitted to the organizations or not.

The consent must be solicited without any deceptive practices, against a privacy notice served to the individuals, and the consent revocation should be as simple as the process of soliciting the consent. Moreover, the individuals need to be explained prior to the solicitation of consent about the consequences of granting and denial of consent. By doing so, the organization is empowering the user to make an informed decision.

Despite the consent withdrawal, the organizations may require retaining certain personal data for a period to comply with legal or contractual obligations.

It is extremely important to note that not every personal data processing is performed because of consent acting as the legal basis, since there may be other laws in place that would require the processing of such data without the consent of the individual.

The consent and choice principle functions in coherence with the accountability principle, where the organization adheres to its requirements for collecting and processing personal data and the conditions for fulfilling the requirements of consent.

4. OPENNESS, TRANSPARENCY & NOTICE

The objective of Openness, transparency and notice is to ensure that individuals are provided with accurate information prior to or at the time of collection or processing of their personal data.

This requires communicating to the individuals about the legal basis for collecting and processing their personal data, as well as the sources from which the data is obtained, whether directly or indirectly. If the data is shared with other parties, either within or outside the jurisdiction, this must also be clearly communicated along with the legal grounds for such disclosures.. It must also entail the rights that the individuals can exercise over the personal data and the manner in which the rights can be exercised.

The organizations can uphold the principle of openness, transparency, and notice through various channels. Still, a Privacy Notice is one of the most common tools that an organization can opt for as it is less resource intensive and easy to spread across the individuals whose personal data is to be processed. The privacy notice must be updated and notified to the users whenever there is a change in the personal data processing activities of the organizations.

The transparency principle demands that the text must be communicated in easy, plain language, avoiding the legalese tone because the legalese tone can impair the ability of the individuals to grasp the conditions for personal data processing. It is not the complexity of the language but the use of technical jargon that often prevents individuals from understanding the terms of personal data processing. Additionally, the length of the Privacy Notice is another cause of concern as individuals can ignore the Privacy Notice merely because of the length of the text.

Woodrow Hartzog, Professor of Law and Computer Science at Northeastern University, in his work highlights this issue, referring to it as a "bandwidth problem." In his research, he notes that if someone were to read every privacy notice for the services they use, it could take up to 76 days each year It is also extremely important that societies that are composed of various diasporas speaking different languages must be able to obtain Privacy Notices in their own language to help them easily understand the complex terms and points of concern.

Transparency is key to ensuring the legitimacy of personal data processing and is pivotal to shifting the power back to the individuals over the personal data that represents them. When individuals are not informed openly and transparently about the legal basis for processing their personal data in plain and easy language, then it deprives them of making an informed decision or seeking a remedy in case of any mishap.

Similarly, when individuals are not provided such information in the language that they understand, then it further accentuates the pain of the marginalized or minority groups within the society.

5. COLLECTION LIMITATION

The principle of Collection limitation is closely knitted with the **Purpose Legitimacy & Specification** Principle. Why? Because it ensures that the collection of personal data remains within the boundaries of what is permitted under applicable laws and justifiable business objectives.

These principles place a check on the organizations to reduce the risk surface to the individuals by ensuring that the personal data is not collected indiscriminately. This means that the organizations must be able to carefully examine the various datasets that they would require to process and consider the social implications of such processing and whether that is justifiable.

6. DATA MINIMIZATION

The principle of Data Minimization is linked with the **Collection Limitation** Principle. While the collection limitation has its focus on the collection of personal data, the minimization is focused on the limitation of processing and data disclosure to other parties.

The principle also acts as a compensating control mechanism to the Collection Limitation to ensure that any indiscriminate PII collected is not processed without a justifiable legal basis.

7. USE, RETENTION & DISCLOSURE LIMITATION

The principle is closely associated with the Purpose Legitimacy principle, which means that the use, retention and further disclosures of personal data must be limited to purposes that have a legal basis.

It is important to reiterate here that the data retention period identified within the Privacy notice is a commitment towards the individuals/data subjects, and hence, the personal data must be securely disposed of at the end of the retention period.

If the organization wishes to retain the personal data indefinitely, then it must be guarded on a sound legal basis, or such personal data must be anonymized.

We will discuss in detail the Personal Data Retention period and its challenges in **Section**.

8. ACCURACY & QUALITY

The Accuracy and quality of personal data are significantly linked to the rights and interests of the individuals, as any damage to the data can deprive individuals of their rights and benefits.

The objective behind the principle is to ensure that the personal data being processed is accurate, updated, and relevant to the identified purpose of processing. The personal data being collected from sources other than the individuals themselves must also be examined for data quality checks.

The validation mechanisms must be embedded within the processing to ensure the quality and correctness of the personal data being processed.

9. INDIVIDUAL ACCESS & PARTICIPATION

The Individual access and participation principle is the cornerstone of the entire discussion around dealing with asymmetric information and power between individuals and organizations. To restore the balance, the individuals must be provided with the avenues and the rights through which they can gain control over their own data or the data that defines them.

Various laws and regulations have provisions to ensure individuals' rights are protected when it comes to personal data. The objective is to give the individual access to their own personal data after a verifiable authentication process.

10. INFORMATION SECURITY

Information security is a cousin of Data Privacy, and there are some thin lines between the two disciplines. However, the information security discipline is broader and is not limited to personal data only. It also ensures that all lawful and proportionate personal data collected is being processed, stored and disclosed in accordance with the information security principles.

Information security ensures that personal data is protected by well-knitted administrative, technical, and physical security controls to ensure the integrity, confidentiality and availability of the personal data.

It is noteworthy that when a personal data breach occurs, it is largely because of inadequate information security hygiene, which may be caused due to unauthorized access, improper destruction, unauthorized disclosure, etc.

It is incumbent upon the organizations to ensure that access to personal data is granted in proportion to their official duties, and a well-designed process is created to provision and de-provision access to the personal data.

11. PRIVACY COMPLIANCE

Every jurisdiction or sector has some laws and regulations that may holistically cover personal data protection or may carry provisions for the protection of personal data. Therefore, it's extremely important to understand the underlying theme of the laws and regulations.

All Laws, regardless of their material scope, are established with a specific spirit and essence, which is enshrined in the provisions, clauses, and regulations.

Without understanding the spirit and essence of Laws and their regulations, we may never be able to truly attain the objectives associated with them.

In times when we see Privacy Laws, regulations, and associated principles blooming, we mustn't just concentrate our discourse on the surface requirements but on the spirit and essence of the Laws.

When the focus is limited to adherence for compliance purposes only, it often creates a mere illusion of compliance, which ultimately drains the essence of the law and leads to its compromise and neglect.

1.4 Data Privacy - Ethical Challenges

Privacy is a Casualty by Default for Poor & Underprivileged

As previously stated, privacy is a fundamental human right that safeguards our other individual rights. It is essential for protecting our dignity, freedom from intrusion, and freedom from judgment. To uphold data privacy, we require robust data protection and security. Unfortunately, marginalized members of society are frequently compelled to sacrifice their privacy in order to secure more immediate basic rights.

I'd like to share my personal experience. A janitor who worked in my office once approached me for help. His residency permit had expired, and he hadn't been paid his salary for over a month. On top of this, his sponsor company instructed him to download a mobile application and log in to accept the organization's terms and conditions to receive his salary and renew his residency. The problem was that the application wasn't in a language he could understand. So, he came to me for help in creating the account and accepting the terms.

While assisting him, I ended up seeing his national ID, salary details, and age. I wasn't comfortable being exposed to this sensitive information and told him so. But for him, getting his residency renewed and receiving his unpaid wages was more important than protecting his personal data.

This made me reflect on how many people from underprivileged backgrounds are used to compromising their privacy and how many even see it as a real issue. Very often, their struggles are so basic and immediate that protecting privacy becomes a luxury they simply can't afford.

In this case, the individual could have been better served if the mobile application supported multiple languages, especially considering the diversity of the labor force expected to use it. Alternatively, a different process could have been designed to ensure that privacy was not compromised and that they have better access to such information and procedures.

This example shows how seemingly small design oversights can have a serious impact on people, especially those already facing difficult circumstances.

Case of Helicopter Research

Helicopter research is a phenomenon that entails research activities targeted toward less prosperous regions and jurisdictions. This often includes the countries of Global South and is sponsored and carried out by researchers from wealthier countries or well-resourced institutions.

Such research initiatives aim to collect data or samples with very little collaboration with local communities, raising ethical concerns about fairness and transparency around personal data collection and processing.

The following challenges often crop up due to such research initiatives:

1. Absence of Appropriate Consent or Misguided Lawful Purpose identification

In poor countries or often countries within the global south, the data privacy regulations may not be fully developed or matured, making it easier to collect and deduce conclusions without proper local involvement. Even if there may exist data protection regulations, the common masses may not understand the significance of their personal data to their lives and the facts of how their personal data may be used, stored or shared without their consent.

2. Data Sovereignty and Ownership Issues

The personal data often collected under such research initiatives is frequently transferred to institutions in other countries, reducing local control over that data. This undermines the concept of data sovereignty—where communities have the right to manage and protect their own data—and can lead to scenarios where the benefits of research are reaped primarily by external entities rather than the local population.

3. Risk of Misuse and Unintended Exposure

Sensitive or personal data may not be adequately anonymized or secured when managed externally. This could increase the risk of data breaches, misuse, or even re-identification of individuals, which could have legal, social, and personal consequences for those involved.

4. Ethical and Long-Term Consequences

Beyond immediate data privacy concerns, helicopter research can contribute to a broader pattern of exploitation. This occurs when research is conducted in communities without meaningful involvement or benefit to those communities. The absence of reciprocal partnerships means that local communities miss the opportunity to build their own research capacities and develop strong data privacy practices, which perpetuates existing inequalities and can erode trust in scientific research.

1.5   Data Privacy as Public Policy Challenge

Public Policy is an instrument that is used by nation states to achieve the aspirations of the nations. The moral codes held and shared together by society compel its policymakers to draft policies, laws, and regulations that represent the ethos and aspirations of society.

Human societies have historically relied on information and data to innovate and create value within society. Banking and financial sector, medical facility providers, and government entities have always relied on information and data to deliver services, create products, and contribute to the overall socio-economic growth of the society. However, the size, structure, and usability of the data have varied throughout human history.

With today's computational and analytical capabilities, there are increasing avenues to develop profiles of human behaviour around their purchasing, spending, and consumption habits, their genetic profiling, their travel history, medical history, etc. While these capabilities add value to human society, they also come with risks of intruding into the privacy of individuals within the society.

Unfortunately, the discourse around personal data is only centred around its protection from leakage or prevention from breach. However, the primary objective to safeguard the personal data is to ensure that such data is not processed to create an unfair society and bring about unfair outcomes.

The amount of discrete data available today allows us to bring more nuance and innovations into public policy, and therefore iron out any imbalances within the society.

The Public policy experts wish to avail the luxury associated with discrete personal data accumulated by public and private organizations to effectively address issues associated with health care, financial sustainability, and overall security concerns.

To put forward any policy recommendations, there is a need to identify broad patterns of human behaviour and propose a solution that may further require some algorithmic decision making. This identification of human behaviour or preferences and then associating it with respect to ethnicities, race, or religion can be a cause to deepen the wedges within a society.

It is therefore that the protection of personal data is not just associated with its secure storage in a safe or information systems but rather its fair processing that helps to eliminate or minimize the asymmetry within the social classes of the society but when such personal data is used to carve out policies that might be extractive in nature or to target a particular section of a society, then there is strong likelihood that it would end up legalizing the prejudice and systemic racism.

There is strong contention among privacy advocates that the use of such discrete personal data can be used to strengthen the elite capture and cultivate extractive public policies, where minorities of the society can be further targeted for extraction.

Consider the scenario where the increasing medical treatment costs need to be addressed within a society and as the public policy makers begin to crunch through the data, they figure out that a substantial chunk of medical costs have been associated with the treatment of a specific disease which might be more prevalent within individuals and families of a specific racial or ethnic background.

If similar information is used by public policy makers or regulatory authorities to allow medical insurance companies to increase the insurance premium for individuals belonging to that racial or ethnic community, then it may put the community at a disadvantageous position or may deprive some from similar communities to afford the medical insurance at all.

There can be various similar scenarios where minority sections of the society can be subjected to policy decisions that will inflict damage to the society's fabric. Therefore, such data processing might serve as a tool to perpetuate the problem rather than the solution.

Another critical aspect is related to Surveillance capitalism, an idea introduced by an American philosopher and social science expert, Shoshana Zuboff, in *The Age of Surveillance Capitalism* (2019). It hinges on the appropriation and commercialization of personal data for reaping business profits. The biggest beneficiaries of such phenomena are the BigTech that have the capabilities to collect, store, and process huge amounts of personal data. Their ability to store and process data further emboldens them to curate such personal data elements for business benefits and thus entrenches their powers over the individuals and the society. Cory Doctorow, a Canadian writer, in his book How to Destroy Surveillance Capitalism argued against the premise of Shoshana Zuboff by establishing an argument which states that the true power of big tech lies in their monopolistic control over markets, not their ability to perfectly manipulate users.

This monopolistic control over the markets enables these organizations to exercise significant power over the individuals, creating an asymmetric power imbalance which is increasingly getting strengthened by the development and acquisition of AI solutions. This concentration of power and control may often lead to market manipulation and digital behavior of the individuals, with a strong likelihood of disrupting economic justice and posing a significant risk to the rights, interests, and freedoms of the individuals.

Cory Doctorow sees **regulation and antitrust laws** as the real solution, rather than assuming companies have magical control over human psychology. It is important to mention here that Transparency is a fundamental principle of privacy, which attempts to offset the asymmetric power imbalance between the big organizations and the individuals or society at large. The organizations, therefore, dispense privacy notices to explain the way the organizations collect and process personal information. However, it may only create an illusion of restoration of balance if the individuals are unable to question the organizational personal data processing activities due to exhaustive processes or due to the legalese language in which the privacy notices are often disseminated.

The objective of personal data processing must be linked to the creation of a fair, harmonious, and a just society.

1.6 Need for Data Privacy Clauses in Modern Laws.

All personal data protection laws or regulatory frameworks require that the organizations collecting and processing   personal data must have an appropriate legal basis for processing the personal data.

As mentioned above, every society is experiencing increased datafication where every aspect of our lives is codified as a data point and once the organizations amass these data points, it would not be difficult to predict that there will be laws created in the future to leverage these data points for the collective interests of society.

Within the realm of Data Privacy, adherence to legal obligations is one of the lawful purpose behind the processing of personal data. It becomes extremely vital that any laws created are privacy-centric, meaning that there are legal provisions within the laws and regulations that uphold the principles discussed in the previous sections of the book that explained the Data Protection principles.

Laws and regulations are eventually a reflection of society and the aspirational values espoused by the society. When societies converge on a certain set of values, then laws and regulations are used as a tool to uphold and protect those common values and interests.

Let's take the example to further deconstruct the idea of fair processing when it might be needed because of an existing law or a regulation. Think of a social media platform that records our time spent on their applications, the kind of content consumed (music, religious lectures, drama, Film, and its genre, adult comedy, political commentary).

The Social media platforms maintain a profile around user consumption habits so that the user is served with content that the person likes to consume. Such data unearths the personal preferences of an individual or can also reveal the value system of the person or the likely shift in the value system of the person.

Before we present a hypothetical scenario, the question that arises is who can obtain such data from these social media companies and for which purposes, and with whom such data can be shared. If such data is to be shared with government agencies, can they make any moral judgments/determinations on such granular data?

What would be the legal provisions that safeguard the rights and freedoms of individuals from government agencies making such moral judgements/determinations? If a government agency acquires that personal data, then is it entitled to share that personal data with other agencies beyond borders, which may also accentuate the transnational repression.

But what if such personal data is owned by private entities, and is traded with other entities, whether private or public entities, for pure commercial purposes?

Now let's consider a hypothetical scenario where a person who regularly listens to Hip-hop Music on an online content platform and after a few months decides to either abandon listening to music or prefers a more melancholic genre for a substantial period. In case the person shifts their preferences towards more political commentary or religious lectures. In this case, how will this shift in preferences or choice be recorded as a datapoint?

If the same person comes under the radar for a government investigation, then would the government agencies have access to such granular information from social media platforms, and under which pretext or law?

If the government agencies can have access to such information under a specific law which aims to preserve the overall benefits of the society, then can the law enforcement agencies make moral judgements/determinations about the individuals based on the granular personal data demonstrating the choices or preferences of a person from drifting away towards melancholic music and political commentary from hip-hop music. Would such a shift in a person's preferences enable the government agencies to build a case for his emotional instabilities, depression, and extremist tendencies?

What's dreadful is how all our thoughts are going to be framed and codified, and how such codification will lead to revocation or dispensation of our rights and responsibilities within the societal structures.

Take the example of Anxiety as an emotion that has a negative connotation, but it acts as a powerful tool as well to keep individuals charged and determined in pursuit of their goals. How individuals are framed because of anxiety can have far more detrimental effects on their lives than anxiety itself.

It is therefore important to ensure that the pretext of the law by virtue of which such data is to be obtained from social media platforms is clearly stated and informed to the end-users. The scope of determinations and their methodology must be clearly set out and explained to the individuals to ensure fairness and transparency around personal data processing. Quite often, the data privacy professionals assume that privacy notices are adequate to ensure transparency. However, such notices are just the means to communicate, the absolute transparency lies in the content being disseminated through the channels.

To summarize, the entities are often processing personal data for the fulfillment of a legal obligation; however, it's extremely necessary that the laws or regulations that empower such processing must also provide a mechanism to protect the rights and freedoms of individuals.

1.7 Moral Underpinnings of the Data Subject Requests.

There exists a peculiar dissonance in our contemporary digital landscape. Organisations deploy increasingly sophisticated mechanisms to collect, analyze, and monetize personal data—machine learning models that predict human behavior, sentiment analysis tools that map emotional responses, and surveillance architectures that track movement through both physical and virtual spaces. Yet when individuals exercise their fundamental right to access this collected information about themselves, they are often met with systems designed for obfuscation rather than transparency, for obstruction rather than illumination.

This contradiction lies at the heart of our modern understanding of Data Subject Access Requests (DSARs), which have quietly evolved from bureaucratic formalities into one of the most potent tools for algorithmic accountability and digital self-determination. The transformation has been both technical and philosophical, reflecting broader shifts in how we conceptualize privacy, autonomy, and power in an age of ubiquitous data collection. Where early data protection frameworks treated access rights as simple transactional obligations, we now recognize DSARs as complex sociotechnical systems that mediate between institutional power and individual agency.

Data subject rights are a critical frontier in digital governance and trust, one where the promises of transparency and accountability either become meaningfully exhibited or are exposed as hollow rhetoric. The implications extend far beyond compliance checklists - they touch on fundamental questions about human dignity, institutional power, and the evolving social contract in data-driven societies.

I. Theoretical Foundations: The Philosophy of Access Rights

Unlike other data rights that focus on restricting processing (e.g., the right to erasure) or controlling future uses (e.g., purpose limitation), access rights are fundamentally about knowledge and understanding.

Early implementations in national data protection laws treated access rights as relatively straightforward informational claims. The OECD Guidelines (1980), for example, framed them primarily in terms of giving individuals "the right to know" about data collection - a formulation that presumed simple, static data systems where the relationship between data collector and data subject was direct and transparent.

This presumption has been thoroughly destabilized by technological change. The rise of complex data ecosystems - where personal information flows through networks of processors, controllers, and third parties, often transforming machine learning and analytics - has rendered the original conception of access rights increasingly inadequate. A dataset about an individual might originate from their own device, be enriched by third-party brokers, processed through proprietary algorithms, and used to make decisions through systems that even their operators struggle to explain.

Contemporary scholarship has begun grappling with these challenges. Wachter (2021) proposes reimagining DSARs as "algorithmic accountability mechanisms" rather than simple information disclosures. Citron and Pasquale (2014) argue for understanding them as tools to combat what they term the "scored society," where opaque algorithmic judgments shape life opportunities. These theoretical advances have yet to fully penetrate practice, creating a gap between what DSARs could be and what they currently are - a gap this chapter seeks to address.

II. DSARs as Sociotechnical Systems: An Original Framework

To properly understand modern DSAR implementation, we must move beyond viewing them as mere legal obligations and instead analyze them as complex sociotechnical systems. Such systems comprise not just technical components (databases, redaction tools, APIs), but also human actors (legal teams, data subjects, regulators), organizational processes, and cultural norms that collectively shape outcomes.

1.8   Data Privacy and Ethics of Artificial Intelligence

The rise of Artificial Intelligence further accentuates the concerns around Privacy and personal data protection. Data acts as a raw material where models are trained on large datasets for the training and testing of machine learning.

One of the foremost concerns associated with AI is around the violation of personal data protection principles, which could embolden avenues for societal harms like discrimination, intrusion, or or the erosion of civil liberties. These risks arise when granular behavioral patterns are unearthed and/or consumed, which can later be used to profile individuals, as mentioned earlier. These issues become further concerning if the society is nudged to provide their personal data in exchange for other material benefits, which may be insignificant, or if they are cajoled to provide the personal data with deceptive practices.

As we mentioned earlier, the importance of personal data is akin to personal hygiene, and understanding of protecting one's own privacy is not uniform among all individuals and the different sections of society.

Issues of Legitimacy & Transparency.

Additionally, the issues of Legitimacy and transparency crop up as the massive personal data that is owned by the private organizations which gives them immense power to make determinations about the individuals and where such determinations or raw personal data is sold to other entities.

This exercise of this power gained through the accumulation or processing of personal data has to earn its legitimacy, for which Transparency is extremely important, as it enables affected individuals to scrutinize determinations and the exercise of power by seeking remedies. If affected individuals are not cognizant of why a decision was made, they cannot seek a remedy or hold the decision maker accountable.

Henceforth, legitimate exercise of power requires that individuals be able to endorse those exercises of power.

Perpetuating Inequality through Unfair Personal Data Processing.

With the increased datafication of society, the importance of context has progressively diminished. Real life demands an intricate understanding of context, social, and economic justice to reach correct conclusions around different facets of life.

We would like to bring to light a scenario of inequality perpetuated and attempted to be automated through an algorithm adopted by a county in Pennsylvania. The Allegheny algorithm is cogently discussed in a book named *Automating Inequality* by Virginia Eubanks, which conducts predictive risk modeling to aid in public welfare systems.

The Allegheny Family Screening Tool (AFST) was developed to assist child welfare caseworkers in Allegheny County, Pennsylvania. It is used to predict the risk of child abuse or neglect. In 1974, the Child Abuse Prevention and Treatment Act was signed to be turned into law by US President Richard Nixon. The Law defined child abuse and neglect as the "physical or mental injury, sexual abuse, negligent treatment, and maltreatment of a child by the person who is responsible for the child's welfare."

The case of the Allegheny Family Screening Tool perfectly depicts the limitations of data points when they are divorced from the social sciences. The ideas of abuse and neglect were very broadly defined in the law, giving the welfare case workers immense latitude to classify a lot of parenting behaviors into the categories of abuse and neglect.

What is important to take into consideration is the fact that when a family is going through a poverty cycle or parental relationship issues and seeking government welfare services, then the children are often subjected to some unwanted and undesired form of neglect due to the lack of fundamental resources.

As Virginia Eubanks points out that the Pennsylvania General Assembly reduced the budget for human services by about 12M USD, which sparked a crisis in a county whose resources were already in decline following the recession of 2007.

The authorities decided to make better use of the datapoints by creating an algorithm that could assist in predictive risk modeling and ensuring allocation of resources to the right recipients. An RFP was raised and the project was eventually awarded to the University of Auckland which proposed to design, develop, and implement a decision-making tool with the capability to mine data within the data warehouse. The expected outputs of the tool were the predictions regarding the children who might be at greater risk of abuse and neglect.

Data Sources

The AFST relied on extensive data collected from various government agencies. Some key sources of data included:

- **Public Welfare Records:** Data on families receiving food assistance (SNAP), Medicaid, or Temporary Assistance for Needy Families (TANF).

- **Juvenile Justice Records:** Information on past interactions of family members with the juvenile justice system.

- **Behavioral Health Records:** Mental health and substance abuse treatment history.

- **Housing and Homelessness Data:** Information on families who received public housing assistance or emergency shelter.

- **Previous Child Welfare Reports:** Prior calls to child protective services (CPS), even if unsubstantiated.

Importantly, the algorithm did **not** incorporate the data of the families that might be taking the support of the nannies and private day care, and not the state resources. While the children of the affluent classes could also suffer from neglect and abuse, their data would never end up in the database to be analyzed by AFST.

How the Algorithm Worked

The AFST functioned as a **predictive risk model** by assigning a risk score (from 1 to 20) to each reported family, with higher scores indicating a greater likelihood of child maltreatment. The algorithm worked as follows:

1. **Data Processing**: When a child welfare report was made, the system pulled relevant data from public records about the family.

2. **Risk Score Calculation**: The algorithm weighed 132 different factors using a statistical model based on historical data. It identified correlations between certain characteristics and past cases of abuse or neglect.

3. **Caseworker Guidance**: The risk score was presented to caseworkers, who could use it to determine whether a case should be investigated further. While caseworkers retained discretion, the algorithm's recommendations strongly influenced decisions.

Expected Advantages

Proponents of the algorithm believed it would:

- **Reduce Human Bias**: By relying on data-driven predictions, it aimed to eliminate subjective decision-making by caseworkers.

- **Improve Efficiency**: The model was expected to help prioritize high-risk cases and allocate resources more effectively.

- **Enhance Child Safety**: By identifying families at high risk earlier, it was believed the system could prevent harm before it occurred.

Adverse Impacts

Virginia Eubanks critiques the AFST, highlighting its potential for reinforcing systemic inequality. Key concerns include:

- **Bias in Data**: Since the model relied on data from public assistance programs, low-income families were disproportionately targeted. Wealthier families, who may also engage in child neglect, were less likely to be flagged because their interactions with social services were minimal.

- **Over-Surveillance of Poor Families**: Families receiving government aid were subjected to more scrutiny than those who did not. This reinforced the idea that poverty itself was a risk factor for child maltreatment.

- **Lack of Community Input**: Families affected by the system had little say in how the algorithm was developed or used.

- **Questionable Accuracy:** Some studies suggested that the algorithm frequently flagged families incorrectly, leading to unnecessary investigations and stress for families who posed little actual risk.

The book *Automating Inequality* perfectly depicts how data becomes a tool to perpetuate inequality and injustice when it is divorced from social context and societal structures. Virginia Eubanks argues that AFST disproportionately impacted marginalized families and perpetuated existing social inequalities. This particular case exemplifies and reinforces how personal data may unconsciously serve as a tool to perpetuate discrimination, systemic injustice, and schisms within society and how it creates a challenge to public policy.

Various jurisdictions also consider certain personal data elements as sensitive or protected characteristics because of their ability to perpetuate harms within the society in the form of Discrimination. Discrimination is not only deemed as an ethical concern but is also illegal in certain jurisdictions, particularly in the UK, where the Equality Act 2010 defined nine protected characteristics, such as gender reassignment, marriage, civil partnership, age, disability, pregnancy and maternity, race, religion or belief, sex or sexual orientation.

It is therefore vital to realize that automated systems may promise efficiency in pruning data and bring out certain facts, but they often reinforce systemic and deep-rooted biases.

SECTION II
DATA PRIVACY
GOVERNANCE

Data Privacy is still a new and niche discipline, and to establish its governance and operating model requires an understanding of the societal challenges that were explained above. Governance is needed to uphold the values enshrined in the Data Privacy laws and regulations. Therefore, it's important that the Privacy Governance and operating model is designed in accordance to protect the rights, freedoms, and interests of the individuals.

The following sections are focused on establishing the governance structures and frameworks that would enable Privacy to transcend from a philosophical idea into operations.

2.1 Reporting Line and Operating Model

Organizations are often faced with the challenge of identifying the best reporting line to where the Data Privacy function must be reporting to. The EU-GDPR and ISO 27701 exhort the need for the Data Privacy function to be independent from competing interests, else it could lead to the compromise of rights, freedoms, and the interests of the individuals.

If the Data Privacy function is residing in the lower layers of the organization, then it may compromise the very principles of personal data protection that need to be upheld.

Before you embark on the journey to establish Governance for Personal Data Protection within your organization, you must determine the reason and governance objectives. Privacy Governance is supposed to uphold the ethical values espoused by your organization and by society at large. These values are often protected and upheld either through internal existing policies or through regulatory and legal instruments within society. It's pivotal to have such clarity to ensure that all services and products offered by your organization offer adequate hygiene to protect the rights, interests, and freedoms of the individuals.

Once this has been determined, it's crucial to identify the functional unit that will be responsible for spearheading the Data Privacy within your organization. To identify the functional unit and its placement within the organizational structure, it's imperative to consider the concept of the 3 lines of defense related to risk governance.

The concept was initially formalized decades ago and adopted by many organizations as the best business practice for risk governance.

The first line of defense is responsible for value creation within the organization and is expected to look for and create opportunities for innovation and disruptions within the market. It includes departments like business development, sales and marketing, product development, HR, and Information technology, etc.

The second line of defense is also known as the control function, and it consists of risk management and compliance functions. These departments or units are tasked with developing risk and compliance management policies, along with their corresponding frameworks, and overseeing the implementation and adherence to risk management practices by the first line of defense.

The third line of defense is an independent audit function that ensures adequate implementation of controls throughout the organization and may involve internal or external resources independent of the organization's business lines and core compliance function.

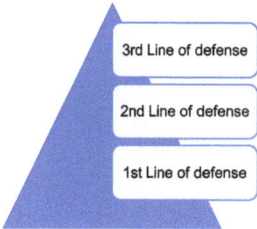

| 3rd Line of defense |
| 2nd Line of defense |
| 1st Line of defense |

While significant privacy by design-related operations and development might be performed by the IT department within the organization but discharging the responsibility of privacy governance to them is counterintuitive because IT essentially provides the muscular power and strength to the organization. Largely, the positioning of the Data privacy function within the first line of defense is going to see the data protection principles dwindle away when there is tough contestation from business and market compulsions.

What is essentially needed is to create a nerve center that understands the complex tangents between data, information security, risk management, data privacy, compliance, legal, and social sciences. Therefore, the thought around the creation of a functional unit should not be centered around monetary resources but largely around competence to navigate the complex terrain across multiple disciplines identified above.

Talking about creating a functional unit to act as a nerve center for privacy governance, the other departments/units operating at the 1st line of defense shall be responsible for providing muscular support for the attainment of data protection principles along with the attainment of business objectives.

It is also important to ensure that such a functional unit is not buried deeper into the organizational structure without adequate access to and oversight of the senior executive management. The results of the data privacy function must be communicated to the oversight management committees and to the relevant board committees. Quite often, the IT department is already overwhelmed with various topics ranging from technology infrastructure, software development, and capacity management, thereby when it comes to providing oversight from the management and the board, the data privacy as a subject may get suppressed in the myriad of issues.

The ideal place for a data privacy function to sit within the organization. Therefore, rests with the departments at the second line of defense that are responsible for establishing risk and compliance management programs. It helps to separate the nerve center from the implementation of privacy governance objectives and subsequently prevents any chances of collusion in eroding the spirit behind the personal data protection principles.

Additionally, the risk and compliance departments are also reporting the progress and challenges to their respective board committees, whether it's an Audit and Compliance committee or a Board risk management committee. As a result, it becomes easier to have the necessary board and management support to implement personal data protection principles through an established data privacy unit.

Organizations may feel intrigued if a standalone functional unit must be created within the risk or compliance department, or responsibility for data privacy should be delegated to an existing unit. There may not be a silver bullet to this question, however, for organizations that are large and geographically dispersed and not having a dearth of resources may find it beneficial to create a stand-alone independent data privacy unit under the auspices of the either risk or compliance department whereas the smaller and medium organizations may find it appropriate to allocate the responsibility of the data privacy function to an existing unit within any of the above mentioned departments after having ensured that all avenues for conflict of interest and collusion are examined and reduced.

The below section highlights the pros and cons of positioning the data privacy responsibilities to either of the below roles.

Chief Information Officer (CIO)

CIOs operate on the first line of defense, which means that they are often responsible for moving fast, providing muscular support by utilizing the data and organizational infrastructure to deliver the business objectives. Their KPIs involve how efficiently they deliver on their targets put forward by the departments, like product management, Human Resources, and others. Data Privacy governance requires managing challenges related to ethics, fairness, transparency, and individual harms. These areas may require professionals with specific expertise in various fields, rather than conventional IT governance.

Placing the responsibility of privacy governance under the sponsorship of the CIO may be a risky proposition, as the interests of data privacy may be suppressed in the race of other competing interests within IT.

Another aspect that needs to be taken into consideration is an effective oversight mechanism; the CIO is usually part of and reports to the strategic progress and challenges to IT steering committees, but not always to some sub-board committees. When it comes to the management committee, the agenda of such committees is already overwhelmed and packed with matters related to software development, capacity management, infrastructure, and technology stack, and therefore, matters related to personal data protection principles may not always yield adequate attention.

CHIEF INFORMATION SECURITY OFFICER (CISO)

Contrary to CIOs, the CISOs operate on the 2nd line of defense and various cybersecurity regulatory instruments profess and enforce the separation of duties between IT and information security with the underlying rationale that Information Security is essentially a control function to ensure that information assets are governed and managed respecting the fundamental principles of confidentiality, integrity, and availability of information.

The information security units could be a considerable choice to be discharged with responsibilities for data privacy since they are already integrated with the information technology at various fronts, including the systems' development lifecycle, change advisory boards, and the integration between the network operations center and security operations center. In various organizations, the CISOs are reporting to Chief Risk Officers, who in turn are reporting to either CEOs or directly to the board. This ensures that information security has access to the highest levels of the organization, whether at the management or board level.

A counter opinion often surfaces against such placement and carries substantial weight, which is that information security is responsible for protecting and upholding the interests of the organization and not necessarily the interests of the individuals or society at large. Their energies and governance frameworks carry an undertone around alignment with the attainment of business objectives. It is for the same reason that personal data protection is now being pushed away from information security by certain regulators across the globe, so that individual rights, freedoms, and interests are not compromised for the sake of organizational benefits.

In the same breadth where data privacy is supposed to protect individuals against the harms, it is beneficial that such conflicts of interest are avoided by not assigning the responsibilities for data privacy governance to the Information Security unit.

Chief Privacy Officer (CPO)/Data Protection Officer (DPO)

Chief Privacy Officers are beginning to carve out their own space away from Information Security, as their primary role is to protect the rights, interests, and freedoms of the individuals whose personal data is in the possession of the organization. DPOs are essentially the individuals or data subjects' ambassadors within the organization. Operating at the 2nd

28

line of defense makes it easier for them to uphold the ethical requirements associated with personal data processing.

In some organizations, the DPOs report to other chiefs, like the Chief Risk Officer, and therefore have easier access to higher echelons of the organization and to the board through periodic reporting to the board risk committee. Considering the above, the Data Protection Officer makes the most compelling case to spearhead the data privacy function.

Additionally, Privacy by design and default is easier to integrate into the systems' development lifecycle, which can be used to ensure that personal data protection requirements are adhered to in the development of any product or service.

As we mentioned earlier, governance is a tool to ensure personal data protection principles are upheld and manifested within the organization. Therefore, the unit responsible for privacy governance must be significantly insulated from the business interests of the organization.

CHIEF LEGAL OFFICER (CLO)

While there is often a tendency to place privacy governance under the Chief Legal Officer, this preference stems from a "safety first" approach, where an organization is risk-averse and aims to avoid potential lawsuits.

However, it remains a risky proposition considering the legal staff is often not equipped with the technological nuance to navigate the complex terrain of IT infrastructure, software development, network security, data science, risk management, and data governance.

Additionally, there are no touchpoints of the legal department within the systems development life cycle. Therefore, integration of privacy by design and default into the systems development lifecycle may remain a challenge. It's also worth noting that once the Privacy risk management framework is developed, it must be integrated with the organizational enterprise risk management, ensuring that all risks above risk appetite are reported to the board. Within the legal department, there are no established risk management frameworks that assess the risk at all, thereby positioning privacy under the legal department would put the framework associated with Privacy Risk Management in jeopardy.

Chief Ethics & Compliance Officer (CECO)

Chief Ethics & Compliance Officer often reports directly to the Board or to the CEO, depending on the organization's sector. The Chief Ethics & Compliance Officer is also part of the control function operating at the 2nd line of defense.

The role of Chief Ethics and Compliance Officer is critical to foster a culture of integrity, ethical values, and accountability within an organization. The Chief Ethics and Compliance Officer helps ensure that the organization operates in a manner that is both ethical and lawful by putting forward ethical principles, educating employees, monitoring compliance, and advising leadership.

Placing the data privacy function under the auspices of CECO makes it easier to advocate personal data protection principles and ensure that all privacy governance frameworks embody those principles.

It is, however, important to be cognizant of the fact that when privacy governance is placed with the CECO, then the privacy risk management framework must also be integrated with the organizational enterprise risk management framework.

While the above section highlighted the various pros and cons of placing data privacy function under different leadership, an organization must assess its circumstances, regulatory obligations, established conventions and best fit prior positioning data privacy function into their organization.

2.1.1 Choosing Appropriate Governance and Operating Model.

Choosing an appropriate governance and operating model for the data privacy function is a crucial aspect that will determine success and the effectiveness of the data privacy program. It becomes even more important in the attainment of compliance with privacy laws and regulations like the Data Protection Regulation (GDPR), California Consumer Privacy Act (CCPA), PIPEDA, etc.

The choice of governance and operating model impacts structure, responsibilities, and authorities defined within the privacy policies and also subsequently affects the implementation and monitoring of the data privacy program across an organization.

There are three primary governance models that can be adopted for the data privacy function by the organizations:

- Centralized Model
- Decentralized Model
- Hybrid Model

Each of these operating models has its benefits, challenges, and are applicable to different kinds of scenarios. The organizations must carefully examine their choice of operating model based on their structure, regulatory requirements, and risk tolerance.

1. Centralized Model

In a centralized model, the privacy policies and their associated frameworks and procedures are defined and governed by a central team stationed within a region which is responsible for developing and executing the privacy procedures, performing impact assessments, compliance with assessments, responding to privacy incidents and breaches across the organization.

Often led by a Chief Privacy Officer or Data Protection Officer (DPO), the data privacy team works with the business units that may be spread across various regions, either within a single jurisdiction or across multiple jurisdictions.

Pros of the Centralized Model

- **Consistent and Homogenous Approach:** Data privacy policies are easier to implement consistently across the organization, offering clarity and certainty to the other business units that may be spread across multiple regions. Uniformity in approach offers a sense of calm to the business units within the organization as they understand that there is only a single source of truth within the organization to look after the data privacy function.

- **Regulatory Compliance:** The centralized model ensures that regulatory compliance requirements across various jurisdictions are considered before developing a privacy program. The compliance assessments performed by the centralized privacy governance unit provide an organization-wide compliance landscape, providing management and the board with assurance that reflects the organization's compliance status across various jurisdictions..

- **Efficiency & Agility in Operations:** A centralized privacy team reduces duplication of efforts, time consumption, ensuring quicker decision-making regarding personal data protection measures.

Challenges of the Centralized Model

- **Inadequate Understanding of Local context:** Organizations that are spread across various jurisdictions and operate in a sector or industry that is heavily regulated may face a challenge as the central privacy unit may not be entirely familiar with the legal landscape and the regulations with tangents to personal data protection. This may result in a scenario where compliance and data privacy programs may be inadequately designed and developed. Additionally, the lack of adequate understanding and context may give a false sense of compliance to the management and the board.

- **Scalability Challenge:** With the increase in business growth, the organizations are naturally expected to expand, and henceforth, a central privacy team may struggle to manage global compliance and local nuances in an effective manner.

- **Slow Response Time:** As the regulatory landscape increases with the expansion of the organization across multiple jurisdictions, the central privacy unit may require more time to examine whether privacy requirements are being fulfilled. This resultantly delays the decision-making as offshore business teams must seek approvals from a central privacy unit, and this may potentially lead to delays in time-sensitive initiatives.

Cost and Budgetary Considerations

- **Capital & Budgetary Requirement:** Centralized operating model requires budget allocation only for a central team, which means that management can allocate human and technical resources centralized with the intent to serve the business units spread across regions within or across jurisdictions.

- **Human Resources & Redundancy:** While it is cost-effective to have a centralized team responsible for the privacy compliance program for all the regions, the centralized team may lack a thorough understanding of the privacy regulations applicable in different jurisdictions. Thus, requiring additional consulting arms located offshore.

Even if the organization can knit along well-meaning and suave privacy experts, there would always be a threat of losing such resources that have a sound understanding of multiple regulations, thereby raising the risk of inadequate and incompetent staff.

Lastly, if the centralized team is overwhelmed, additional resources may be required to manage operations at scale, which may further require additional budgetary support.

Appropriate Fit:

- Organizations operating in heavily regulated industries like **finance and banking, airlines, healthcare, and pharmaceuticals.** Central oversight is essential to ensure the organization adheres to all regulatory obligations related to personal data protection.

- Organizations that operate within a **single jurisdiction** or carry a **homogeneous business model** that does not require privacy approaches tailored to different jurisdictions.

- Startups or mid-sized organizations that require a strong foundational privacy framework, however, as they begin to scale, they must re-examine their governance and operating model for efficacy.

2. Decentralized Model

In a decentralized model, privacy governance is distributed across regions and jurisdictions. Each jurisdiction has its own chief privacy officer or data protection officer responsible for developing and executing a data privacy program in alignment with the applicable laws and regulations relevant to that jurisdiction.

In a decentralized governance model, an organization establishes different privacy teams to look after different regions or jurisdictions, like having a dedicated team and DPOs for the European region, a dedicated DPO for the Middle Eastern region, and a separate DPO for North America.

Pros of the Decentralized Model

- **Local Nuance & Context:** Privacy programs are developed based on legal and regulatory instruments pivotal to that region or jurisdiction's coverage. A decentralized approach helps to cut the clutter and tricky overlapping between various regulations tied across jurisdictions, such as privacy regulations for the Middle East, Europe, North America, the Australian continent, etc.

- **Operational Agility:** With a decentralized approach, it's easier to focus energies only on the regulations tied to the applicable region or jurisdiction, and such localized decision-making enables the organization to make quicker decisions and support the business pursuits.

- **Scalability:** An organization that enjoys presence across multiple continents and jurisdictions will find it easier to scale as the dedicated DPOs and their team will be able to pursue business pursuits in alignment with applicable privacy laws and regulations of that jurisdiction.

Challenges of the Decentralized Model

- **Inconsistencies in Privacy compliance:** Decentralized governance model may lead to circumstances where different regions may not have similar fundamentals in carving out a data privacy program, and resultantly, the privacy compliance status of the organization will be affected. It could be the case where a privacy office looking after affairs of the European region might be far more mature and advanced in its execution of a privacy program than the privacy office in the North American region, and this will lead to an inconsistency in the implementation of a privacy program.

  It must be considered that often, the fire of non-compliance and penalties invoked in a specific region affects business activities and their pursuits even in other regions. For example, if an organization that has its presence across the globe and was penalized for non-compliance with privacy regulations in the European region, then its business in the Middle Eastern region and other regions may also be affected.

- **Inadequate Oversight:** The executive management and the board may not be able to correctly ascertain the current state of privacy operations across the organization, causing the subject of data privacy to be pushed down the organizational layers and absent from the board of directors' horizon.

Cost and Budgetary Considerations

- **Higher operational costs:** Establishing multiple privacy offices and teams across the regions and jurisdictions entails increased costs as capable and competent privacy staff need to be hired for each region, and the necessary technological solutions need to be procured and implemented for effective privacy operations.

- **Variable compliance costs:** Different regions and jurisdictions have different privacy laws and regulations, which also vary in their maturity and depth. This may lead to variable costs of attaining privacy compliance among different regions and may be mistakenly compared for efficiency and cost by the executive management. The Boards might question the variation around the cost of privacy compliance in different regions or jurisdictions, and it may occur due to the varying needs of privacy laws and regulations between jurisdictions. A nuanced understanding of these dynamics is pivotal to maintaining the confidence of the management and board.

Appropriate Fit:

- **Multinational corporations** operating in diverse regulatory environments where a single privacy office cannot manage all compliance requirements.

- Organizations with autonomous subsidiaries operating either in the same or in different industries.

3. Hybrid Model

A hybrid governance model combines aspects of a centralized and a decentralized operating model. The central privacy office, also known as headquarters, establishes policies, frameworks, and compliance programs, while regional privacy offices or business units execute those policies and frameworks within their jurisdiction in accordance with the applicable laws and regulations.

In such circumstances, the central privacy office may develop an overarching data privacy program factoring in all privacy laws and regulations applicable to the organization across all jurisdictions, while the regional offices or business units are mandated to follow the requirements in accordance to the applicable regulations. The regional privacy offices are expected to report privacy compliance to the central headquarters for aggregated reporting to the senior management or to the board of directors.

Advantages of the Hybrid Model

- **Equilibrium between Control and Agility**: The central headquarters develops policies and provides governance, whereas the regional office adapts privacy policies to their needs, ensuring better, nuanced decision-making and agility of operations.
- **Ability to Scale**: Organizations are better equipped to manage privacy operations through regional execution.
- **Better Compliance Management**: Centralized oversight ensures consistency in the privacy governance and policy requirements, while decentralized execution ensures adherence to local regulations.

Challenges of the Hybrid Model

- **Inadequate Coordination**: Managing privacy offices and the implementation of privacy policies and procedures requires clarity in roles, responsibilities, and communication between headquarters and regional teams.
- **Potential Conflicts**: Differing interpretations of policies can create inconsistencies in execution.
- **Resource Intensive**: Needs investment in governance structures, training, and technology to manage privacy across various jurisdictions.

Cost and Budgetary Considerations

- **Moderate to high costs**: Balancing central governance with localized execution requires funding for both. An organization may have to invest in privacy management tools, automation within HQ, and the regional offices as well. However, it also provides an opportunity to reduce the cost by centralizing the aspect of privacy governance to HQ, while the implementation is left to regional offices.

Best Suited For:

- **Large enterprises** and conglomerates with diverse operations and the need to adhere to multiple privacy regulatory instruments.

Organizations must also periodically reassess their privacy governance model with the change in privacy regulations and business evolution.

Which governance model should our organization adopt?

Centralized Model

Ideal for strict
compliance oversight

Decentralized Model

Suits large, diverse
organizations needing
flexibility

Hybrid Model

Balances enterprise-
wide governance with
regional execution

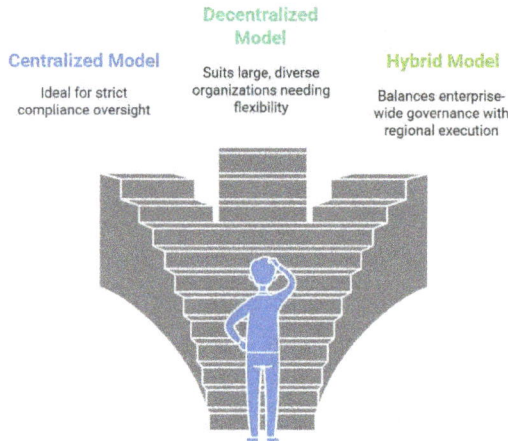

The selection of the right operating model is critical for ensuring privacy compliance, managing privacy risks, and yet maintaining operational agility to support the business pursuits. It is therefore imperative that the operating models are aligned with business goals, regulatory requirements, and internal capabilities because the operating model will play a significant role in building consumer trust and competitive advantage within the increasingly competitive digital economy.

2.2 Why Data Privacy should be a concern for Boards

Before we unearth the importance of Data Privacy to the Board of Directors, we must reinforce the idea that the **Board of Directors act as lynchpin** in corporate governance, where their decisions and judgements not only influence the success or failure of organizations but also the overall stability of the economy and society at large.

The Board of Directors are expected to demonstrate ethical conduct, establish sustainable governance objectives that prevent financial risks, promote sustainable growth, ensure regulatory compliance, and foster trust within society. It is therefore that failure at the board level can have a spiral effect not only on the organization but towards society at large.

With the increased datafication of societies and the ability to codify every human experience, organizations are better equipped to leverage such data for their growth. In fact, it is improbable to create value or engage in trade without intersecting with personal data. If the governance objectives set by the board fail to emphasize the importance of consumer protection, individual rights, and regulatory compliance, there is a strong likelihood that these principles will only be superficially addressed by the organization. In such cases, the value created by the organization will not endure, and the entire foundation of growth will remain unstable.

The board of directors owes a fiduciary duty to their organization, demonstrating utmost loyalty and unscrupulous honesty. The directors and senior management exercise a high degree of control over organizational operations and corporate affairs. Therefore, there is an expectation from such officials at higher echelons to demonstrate competence, integrity, and commitment.

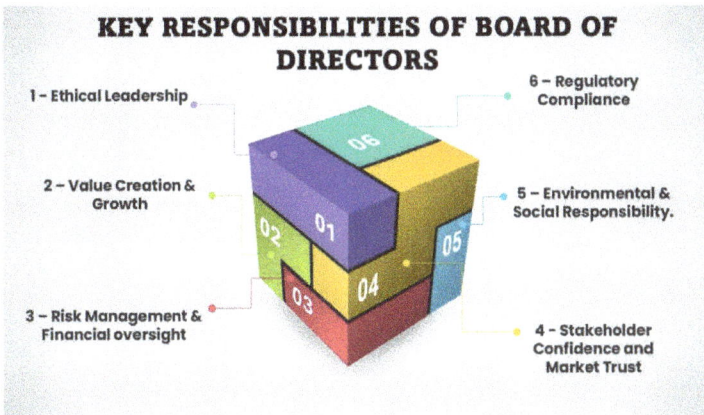

KEY RESPONSIBILITIES OF BOARD OF DIRECTORS

1 - Ethical Leadership

2 – Value Creation & Growth

3 – Risk Management & Financial oversight

4 - Stakeholder Confidence and Market Trust

5 – Environmental & Social Responsibility.

6 – Regulatory Compliance

The image below summarizes the key responsibilities of the Board of Directors. But the most important intersection with regards to this book rests with the responsibility to ensure Regulatory Compliance, and hence comes the need to comply with personal data protection laws and regulations within the jurisdictions. Failure to comply with regulations can result in lawsuits, large fines, penalties, and business disruptions. An independent and competent board ensures that companies remain compliant, reducing legal risks and ensuring that value created by the organization is sustainable and deemed worthy by society at large.

The Board of Directors must exact the progress reports on the below from the management to ensure that there is adequate oversight being exercised to ensure adherence to privacy laws, regulations, and standards.

ITEMS	RATIONALE
Data Privacy Program/Strategy	Helps to ensure that management has developed a formal data privacy strategy or a program that is adequately sponsored through monetary and human resources. The relevant sub-board committee must examine if the data privacy program is on track and if there are any limitations and challenges to the pursuit of the data privacy program. Another key component that the sub-board committee must ensure is whether the Data Protection Officer (DPO) and privacy teams have adequate authority, budget, technical tooling, and staffing to govern operations.
Privacy Risk Landscape	The board must be cognizant of privacy risks that may be lurking within the organizational system. These risks may occur due to existing business pursuits of the organizations where products are collecting disproportionate personal data from the individuals or might be sharing data with jurisdictions deemed inadequate by regulatory authorities. Such information may be presented to the organizational board risk committee to enable them to understand and address the potential consequences of privacy risks on operations, reputation, and compliance obligations. The board of directors must also ensure that the organization has established a formal privacy risk management framework, which is integrated within the organizational frame. Risk Management Framework: Review how privacy risks are identified, assessed, and mitigated within the organization's risk management frameworks and processes and the

	enterprise risk management framework. This ensures that privacy risks are identified, assessed, treated, tracked, reported, and communicated following a formal and approved mechanism rather than an ad-hoc approach.
Privacy Compliance Landscape	The sub-board committee responsible for providing oversight into privacy governance must be served with the organizational compliance status vis-à-vis personal data protection regulatory obligations. This ensures that organizational ethos incorporates adherence to applicable data protection laws such as GDPR, CCPA, HIPAA, PIPEDA, KSA PDPL, etc.
Organizational Privacy Policy	The organizational policies reflect the aspirations and values to be pursued by the organization. When the board approves the Privacy policy of directors, it signals the importance of personal data protection to the success of the organization. Therefore, the board becomes more sensitive to adherence to the privacy policy by the management. Additionally, the approval of the privacy policy by the board facilitates in acquisition of adequate resources, which are essential to create an organizational culture, and they also help in enforcement by ensuring that privacy violations result in clear consequences.
Audit Observations vis-à-vis Privacy	The board of directors are also responsible for providing oversight, and therefore they are entitled to know about the internal and external audit findings that may put the organization at stake. Usually, the Audit and Compliance Committee reports the audit findings to the board members. Reporting such findings to different committees of the board helps to ensure that there is an organizational plan to remediate the gaps identified within the audit observation.
Penalties & Fines Imposed by Regulator	The sub-board committees of the board must be briefed about the penalties, fines, and lawsuits filed against the organization. This helps the board of directors within the committee to carry

	out their fiduciary responsibility to understand the underlying causes and to exhort the management to develop a management action plan to mitigate such occurrences in the future.
Privacy Risk Appetite & Breaches.	The enterprise risk management function maintains the privacy risk appetite statements, and if the thresholds are crossed, then the Board risk committee must be apprised of the details, as ensuring risk oversight is one of the key responsibilities of the board of directors.

The above agenda items provide confidence to society that the organization takes privacy seriously and ensures that there is adequate oversight being exercised by the independent board of directors. When the board of directors exercises their sound independent judgment and expertise from the top, then it facilitates the implementation of personal data protection principles within the fabric and the culture of the organization.

MINIMUM SKILLSETS NEEDED FOR BOARD PERSONNEL TO EXERCISE OVERSIGHT OVER DATA PRIVACY.

Richard Leblanc, Professor of Governance, Law and Ethics, professes that the 3 attributes are quintessential for a board of directors to be valuable. These 3 attributes are Independence, competency, and behavior that make a director effective. He professes in his work for Board governance that if any one of the attributes is weak, then that will impair the board's ability to exercise its responsibilities in a diligent manner. We will unpack the attribute of competence within this book to help organizations determine the qualifications of a competent director to provide oversight related to data privacy.

ATTRIBUTE OF COMPETENCE

While Independence and behavior might be easier to find in a Board of Directors, it is the competence which is critical in most scenarios to ensure that the director is able to grasp the nuances of the privacy laws and regulations and their implications on the business. As we discussed, privacy is still a niche area that requires an understanding of legal, information security, technology, and business understanding. Therefore, it is often challenging to find directors who can have a thorough and in-depth understanding of all these fields. There have been numerous stories in which the failure of the boards was not caused due to the independence of the directors or their behavior, but by the lack of adequate and deep expertise in the subject. It is imperative that the board committee to which data privacy progress is reported has directors who are experts in the field of law, risk management, information security, and technology at large. Such a problem is even more pronounced in societies where the appointment to the board of directors is by virtue of certain entitlement or association to a specific group (nationality or race, etc.) rather than competence. Jurisdictions often have varying mechanisms to assess and validate the competence of the aspiring board of directors. The objective of these mechanisms is to ensure the creation of competent boards rather than simply independent boards.

Any individual's competency is identified through a collection of skills, knowledge and understanding, experience, education, and training within the specific field.

PARAMETERS TO GAUGE COMPETENCE OF DIRECTORS IN THE FIELD OF PRIVACY	
Knowledge & understanding	• Understanding personal data protection principles, Privacy laws, regulations, and standards like GDPR, CCPA, PIPEDA, DIFC Data Protection Law, KSA PDPL, and ISO 27701's structure, etc. • Such knowledge and understanding can be attained through reading regulations and investing in educational and training efforts discussed below.
Skills	• Deal with the ability to practically apply knowledge and skills to different scenarios like conducting Data Protection Impact Assessments, developing privacy notices, establishing Records of Processing activities, and performing Transfer impact assessments. • A director who has never indulged in carrying out these assessments and is only aware of the privacy lexicon will only be able to offer an illusion of competence resultantly leading to poor oversight when to protection of individual rights.
Experience	• Exposure gained over the years through real-world application and implementation in the realm of privacy is always invaluable because once a professional has an adequate understanding of personal data protection principles and has worked at applying those principles, only then can such a professional be appropriately able to provide direction and oversight. Such an individual is equipped to anticipate challenges around international developments likely to affect trade and personal data exchanges and is,

	resultantly able to make informed decisions and mitigate risks.
	• Experience comes from working in privacy-related roles where one learns from one's successes and failures, and has experience in engaging with regulators and stakeholders.
Education & Training	• Pertains to the formal learning and development channels and institutions that impart knowledge and understanding in the form of a university degree or professional certifications like CIPP/E, CIPM, CDPSE, or Fellow of Information Privacy, etc. • Academic courses and corporate training programs provide structured learning and development pathways to ensure that professionals have appropriate education and training.

The functional arms of corporate governance often keep track of their existing Board of Directors competencies through a Competency matrix chart. Such matrix charts help them to understand the current capabilities of their board of directors and facilitate them in identifying the competency gaps within their existing board of directors. Such tools can be leveraged to build the competency of their Board of Directors. It is critical to note that the existing designations of the directors cannot and must not be deemed as the competency, and their presence on the boards of other organizations does not lend credibility to their competence.

ESSENTIAL TRAITS FOR COMPETENT BOARD OF DIRECTORS

1. Independent Thinking: A competent director must also be able to display the independence of judgment by demonstrating impartiality and refraining from engaging in management activities. This even requires directors to express unpopular opinions within the board.

2. Integrity & Loyalty: The directors are responsible for ensuring that individuals' rights are respected and protected by the organization in pursuit of their business objectives. Therefore, the director's own integrity, expressed through trustworthiness, honesty, and consistency in conduct and values, is of paramount importance. When directors demonstrate their commitment to high ethical standards, they are better equipped to uphold the rights, freedoms, and interests of the individuals whose personal data is being processed by the organizations.

3. *Capacity to Contest Ideas*: The director must be capable of challenging and contest ideas, beliefs, and fundamental assumptions of an organization in their pursuit of business interests. Such capacity is only attained through sheer competence, where a director is able to critically evaluate and examine the information at all layers and constructively questions, challenges, and scrutinizes the power being exercised over the individuals through the processing of personal data.

4. *Capacity to Act*: The director must exhibit the willingness and capacity to act when personal data protection principles are being violated, and privacy objectives are not being met. This often leads to tough and difficult conversations because, as a director, one has to be assertive in upholding the privacy principles.

5. *Conceptual & Systems Thinking Skills*: The director must exhibit the ability to solve problems or offer solutions. This can be done if the director has the intellectual capacity to understand, dissect, combine, and interpret complex and diverse information.

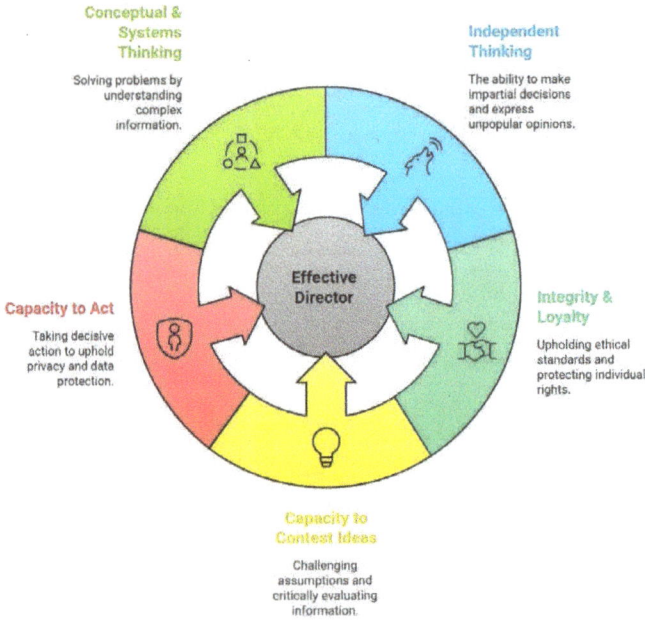

Essential Traits for Effective Directors

Conceptual & Systems Thinking
Solving problems by understanding complex information.

Independent Thinking
The ability to make impartial decisions and express unpopular opinions.

Capacity to Act
Taking decisive action to uphold privacy and data protection.

Effective Director

Integrity & Loyalty
Upholding ethical standards and protecting individual rights.

Capacity to Contest Ideas
Challenging assumptions and critically evaluating information.

Figure 5 ESSENTIAL TRAITS FOR COMPETENT BOARD OF DIRECTORS

2.3 ESTABLISHING A DATA PRIVACY PROGRAM

Once a data privacy or personal data protection unit has been established under the auspices of executive management within any of the above-mentioned leadership positions, it is essential to initiate efforts to equip them with authority and resources to ensure that personal data protection principles are meaningfully pursued and achieved.

2.3.1 Considerations for Establishing a Privacy Program

The Data privacy program must be established with some fundamental considerations and inputs that will act as guardrails and benchmarks for the program. The fundamental considerations and inputs that may assist in developing the data privacy program include the following:

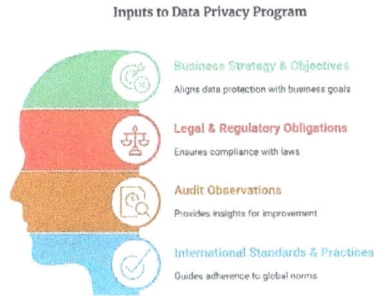

Inputs to Data Privacy Program

Business Strategy & Objectives
Aligns data protection with business goals

Legal & Regulatory Obligations
Ensures compliance with laws

Audit Observations
Provides insights for improvement

International Standards & Practices
Guides adherence to global norms

Figure 6: Inputs to Data Privacy Program

1. Business Strategy & Objectives:

The first and foremost consideration to develop a privacy program will be business objectives and the organizational strategy that will determine the path that the data privacy unit will have to take to develop a privacy program.

This must include the nature of business, products and services offered by the organization, the clientele of the organization, the geographic spread of the organization, and most importantly, the industry and sector in which the organization operates. Specific sectors have more risk propositions attached to them in comparison to others, and therefore their regulatory obligations are often more stringent. Such includes financial, health, and pharmaceutical sectors.

It is important to note that alignment with the business strategy and objectives is vital to the data privacy program. However, that does not mean that the personal data protection principles are watered down to assist the objectives of the organization. One aspect that must never be forgotten within the minds of the data protection officers is that the privacy function is supposed to champion the rights, interests, and freedoms of the data subjects, as often espoused within regulatory instruments and international standards.

2. Legal & Regulatory Obligations:

This will be a key determinant in establishing a privacy program because the legal and regulatory obligations incumbent on the organizations are critical. Often, the non-compliance with regulatory obligations may push the regulatory authorities to revoke the licenses for businesses to operate.

The data privacy section or unit must work with their counterparts in the compliance division to determine the legal and regulatory obligations vis-à-vis privacy that are applicable to the organization.

Regulatory instruments like GDPR, HIPAA, PIPEDA, CCPA, etc., may be applicable to the organizations that need to be factored into developing any privacy program. Additionally, the data privacy team must also factor in any other laws and regulations that are applicable to the organization and might contain privacy provisions and requirements. Such instruments are not privacy-centric per se but carry the provisions and requirements that intersect with privacy.

3. Audit observations.

The organizations have often undergone internal and external audits, which unearth the gaps in the organization related to the protection of personal data. When such gaps are identified and formalized in the form of the report, and are expected to be closed within a given timeframe.

Often, such gaps are related to non-compliance with regulatory instruments or failing to adhere to industry's best practices.

The data privacy unit must encapsulate such requirements and blend them into the data privacy program to ensure that the audit observations are closed simultaneously along with the pursuit of data privacy strategic initiatives.

4. International Standards & Practices.

The organization can benefit from aligning its data privacy program with the international standards and best practices like ISO 27701 Privacy Information Management Systems, Fair Information Practices, Generally Accepted Privacy Principles (GAPP), etc.

This becomes even more important when the organizations are operating in a critical industrial sector and when there are no legal or regulatory instruments within the jurisdiction to force the organization to adhere to personal data protection.

As organizations choose to adhere to international standards and best practices, they display a commitment to the protection of personal data principles and help to earn trust in the minds of data subjects.

The layout below presents a sequential representation of steps that must be taken by the data privacy function to establish a data privacy program.

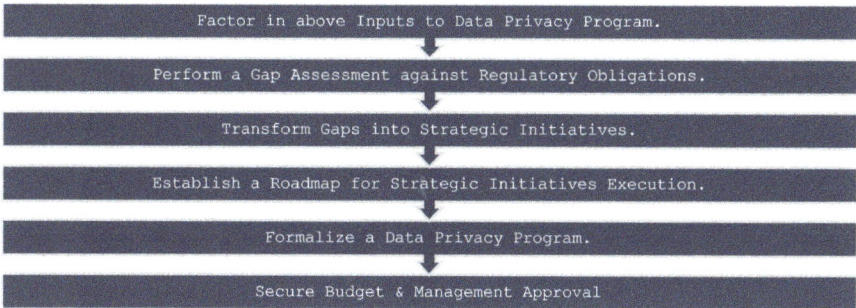

The Data Privacy Program must aim to establish functional capabilities and competencies to ensure that privacy impact assessments are duly performed, incidents and breaches are identified and managed, compliance and audit evaluations are periodically carried out, the employee training and awareness are conducted in a planned and consistent manner.

The figure below identifies the key components of any data privacy program, and the following sections will attempt to cover them.

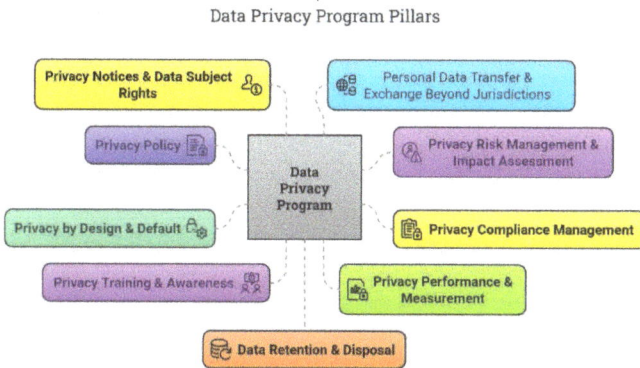

Figure 7 Data Privacy Program Pillars

2.3.2 Data Privacy Policy

The first step in establishing such a program is to define a Data Privacy policy, which shall entail the powers granted to the individual responsible for running the Privacy governance program. The policy must be approved by either the Chief Executive or the equivalent of the organization or by the Board of Directors of the organization. Having a data privacy policy and

47

program approved by the Board of Directors gives the signal within the organization that personal data protection is not established just for window dressing, but it's an area related to which progress and challenges will be reported to the Board.

The individual responsible for establishing and maintaining a privacy governance program must derive their powers and responsibilities from such a policy. Therefore, it's essential that policies capture the authorities and responsibilities.

The Privacy Policy enshrines the strategic path that the organization aspires to undertake in upholding the personal data protection principles. The Privacy policy must be clear, crisp, and convey a directional tone, sense of affirmation, and commitment from the organizational senior management and the board. In addition, the policy statements must be actionable, measurable, and easily accessible to organizational employees and vendors.

Some of the key aspects that must be encapsulated within the organizational privacy policy include:

- **Responsibility, Authorities & Reporting Line.**
  The Data Privacy policy must contain the major authorities conferred to the Data Protection Officer. It must be considered that the policy maintains the essence and spirit of independence that the Data Protection Officer or Chief Privacy Officer must enjoy.

If the authorities of the Data Protection Officer are diluted within the privacy policy, then it will only create an illusion of independence. It is therefore pivotal that the DPO is insulated from any operational conflicts. We must remember that the DPO is essentially an ambassador of the individuals' rights, freedoms, and interests within the organization. Therefore, the DPO must have sufficient independence and authority to ensure that their governance frameworks, processes, and procedures are effective in upholding these rights. The EU's GDPR protects DPOs from being dismissed or penalized by their respective organizations for carrying out their duties, which is a crucial safeguard that enhances security and raises the expectations placed on the DPO..

The data privacy policy must express firm support and conviction to the data privacy unit, ensuring that the unit/department or section is equipped with the necessary budget and resources to develop and operationalize its governance procedures and processes.

Organizations may choose to mention the reporting line of the Data Protection officer within the privacy policy or may develop a stand-alone privacy governance framework, which shall entail details like the reporting line and the operating model of the data privacy unit.

The policy must also capture whether the data privacy function will be reporting its progress and challenges to any oversight committee at the executive management or board level. This shall ensure that adequate measures are taken from the governance perspective to put personal data protection on the horizon of the senior management and the board.

- **Adherence to Personal Data Protection principles.**

The Data privacy policy must exhibit organizational commitment to upholding personal data protection principles, which can be expressed in the following manner, which reflects a non-exhaustive list:

- Personal data shall only be processed in a fair and lawful manner.
- Personal data shall be obtained only for specified, explicit, lawful, and legitimate purposes, and shall not be further processed in any manner incompatible with those purposes.
- Personal data shall be adequate, relevant, and not excessive in relation to the purposes for which they are collected and/or processed.
- Personal data shall be accurate, complete, and current as appropriate for the purposes for which they are collected and/or processed.
- Personal data shall not be kept in a form which permits identification of the Data Subject for longer than necessary for the permitted purposes.
- Appropriate physical, technical, and procedural measures shall be implemented to:
  - *Detect/ Prevent unauthorized or unlawful collection, processing, or disclosure of personal data.*
  - *Prevent accidental loss or destruction of, or damage to, personal data.*
- Privacy Risk Management & Impact Assessment.

The Data Privacy policy must assign the responsibility to establish a Privacy risk management framework that shall drive the activities to conduct a privacy impact assessment exercise. The data privacy policy must encapsulate the scenarios in which the privacy impact assessments must be conducted.

The Privacy Unit must establish its own Privacy Risk Management framework with a Privacy lexicon and taxonomy to equip and facilitate conducting a Privacy Impact Assessment.

- **Personal Data Identification and Management.**

The identification, inventorying, and cataloging of personal data are extremely important and aid further in the dispensation of data subject rights. The data privacy policy must lay down the roles and responsibilities of specific organizational units for appropriately identifying, inventorying, and cataloging the personal data.

- **Security of Personal Data.**

The data privacy policy must express how the organization will look after the security of personal data through administrative and technical measures. Some sample policy statements regarding the protection of personal data may include:

- The organization shall implement adequate technical and organizational safeguards, in line with applicable regulatory requirements to ensure the security of personal data, including the prevention of their alteration, loss, damage, unauthorized processing or access, having regard to the state of the art, the nature of the data, and the risks to which they are exposed by virtue of human action or the physical or natural environment.
- The organization shall ensure that its employees and contractors adhere to information security policies, practices, and any additional guidance issued around personal data protection.
- Employees and vendors involved in any stage of processing personal data shall explicitly be subject to protecting the confidentiality of the Personal Data even after the end of such person's occupational or contractual relationship.
- Employees, contractors, and third-party vendors shall have access only to the personal data necessary for the fulfillment of their employment/ contractual duties.

- **Privacy Compliance Management.**

The data privacy policy must assign responsibility for the privacy functional unit to establish a data privacy compliance framework. The objective of the framework must be to periodically review and monitor organizational compliance vis-à-vis privacy laws and regulations.

- **Privacy by Design & Default.**

The data privacy policy must also encapsulate the need to integrate privacy within the organizational systems' development lifecycle and within the project management lifecycle. This will ensure that all products and services launched by the organization have privacy capabilities baked into them rather than laid on top just for window dressing.

- **Personal Data Transfer & Disclosure Outside Jurisdiction.**

The privacy policy must express the organizational commitment to ensure that any personal data transfer and disclosures made outside the organizational jurisdiction will be within the boundaries of existing privacy laws and regulations.

- **Privacy Training & Awareness.**

The privacy policy must enunciate the importance of training and awareness, and how the organization will allocate resources and budget to ensure cultivation of a privacy-centric culture within the organization and to ensure that the organizational staff is educated and equipped to implement privacy across various layers of the organization.

The privacy policy must allocate responsibility to the relevant organizational unit to develop the training plan for data privacy, and the privacy functional unit must be held responsible for the development of the awareness program.

Some of the possible privacy policy statements in the realm of privacy training and awareness could include.

- The organization shall ensure the development and delivery of the Data Privacy training and awareness program.
- The Privacy governance function shall ensure that awareness materials are periodically reviewed and updated with the latest content in accordance with applicable laws and regulations.
- The privacy governance function shall ensure that privacy awareness activities are conducted annually for staff.
- The effectiveness of the training and awareness program shall be periodically measured and reported.
- **Privacy Performance Assessment.**

The privacy policy must also assign the responsibility of the data privacy unit to develop the privacy functional KPIs and metrics to be reported to relevant management stakeholders within the organization.

- **Data Subject rights.**

The privacy policy must enunciate the data subject rights afforded to the individuals and the organizational commitment to dispense those rights.

The privacy policy may also identify the time period during which the data subject rights will be dispensed, which is often in accordance with privacy regulations. However, the aspect of time-period may also be covered in a stand-alone procedural document.

- **Privacy Notice**

The privacy policy must express a commitment to issue a privacy notice to the individuals for all personal data processing activities undertaken by the organization. Some of the possible privacy policy statements could include.

- The organization shall ensure that Privacy Notices are published across all applicable communication channels.
- The organization shall ensure that Privacy Notices are periodically reviewed to ensure their effective coverage & relevance with a changing environment.

- The organization shall provide a concise, transparent, intelligible, easily accessible, and adequate notice to the Data Subject in physical or electronic format.
- **Choice & Consent.**

The privacy policy must express its firm commitment to ensure that individuals are given a fair choice, and their consent is obtained in a transparent and fair manner without any impression of deception.

Some examples of the policy statements with regard to choice and consent are as follows:

- Consent shall adhere to the principle of a freely given, specific, informed, and unambiguous indication of the data subject.
- The organization shall ensure that the choices provided to the data subject are complete and clear, along with options to opt out.
- The organization shall inform data subjects of the consequences for failing to consent or to provide their data.
- The organization shall obtain new consent if personal data is used for a purpose other than originally disclosed to the data subject.
- **Use, Retention & Disposal**

The privacy policy must affirm the organizational commitment to the principles of Data minimization by ensuring that personal data is used for lawful purposes and is not retained beyond a defined and committed period for the individuals.

2.3.3 Oversight Committee.

Once an organizational unit is identified for managing data privacy function and once its policy has been established, it's essential to create an executive management oversight committee with adequate representation from the organizational management to review progress, deliberate, and provide any support to mitigate the challenges associated with the attainment of privacy governance objectives.

If the Compliance Department is authorized to establish and manage privacy governance functional capabilities, then it's better to extend the reports to sub-board committees like Audit and Compliance. Whereas if the privacy unit is established under the Risk Management Department, then the reports of privacy governance can also be extended to the board risk committee, which is a sub-board committee constituted to examine the organizational risks.

As you embark on establishing the management executive committee to provide oversight of the AI governance function, the following aspects shall hold importance to ensure that such committee is effective:

1. Responsibilities and Authorities granted to the committee.
2. Committee Members
3. Adequate convening of such committee meetings.
4. Ensuring that committee resolutions are well documented, disseminated timely and actioned upon.

To establish a Data Privacy management committee, a charter needs to be established that details the responsibilities and authorities of the management committee. The charter must be recorded within the organizational delegate of authority and must be approved by the organizational corporate governance department. The charter must detail the responsibilities of the committee secretary, members with voting rights, requirements for meeting frequency, the minimum quorum needed for holding a committee meeting, and the manner in which a committee shall make a decision.

The ultimate objective of the committee must be to uphold and manifest the personal data protection principles through its decision-making.

The following table helps to explain the potential members whose presence can be invaluable for the data privacy management committee. It is noteworthy that the inclusion of members may vary from organization to organization. However, it's important to identify individuals looking after these interests in your organization, as they can be beneficial for providing oversight.

MEMBER	RATIONALE
Chief Executive Officer (Equivalent)	Highly instrumental in setting the tone at the top. Having the CEO as part of the oversight committee helps to drive the data privacy program by better mobilization of resources. In some cases, the CEO of the organization may delegate the authority to some other chiefs to act as the chairman of the data privacy management committee.
Chief Risk Officer	Responsible for providing insights and guidance on the privacy

	risks landscape of the organization and how some of the privacy risks may be breaching the organizational risk appetite, thereby ensuring proper reporting even at the Board of Directors level.
Chief Compliance Officer	Responsible for providing insights about the regulatory compliance obligations of the organization vis-à-vis personal data protection.
Chief Privacy Officer/Data Protection Officer.	Responsible for the execution of the data privacy program and for ensuring that business initiatives pursued by the organization do not compromise the rights, freedoms, and interests of the individuals. Chief Privacy Officers/Data Protection Officers, being the beacon of individual rights within the organization, ensure that the organization conforms to the privacy laws, regulations, and privacy risk management practices.
Chief Information Security Officer	The Chief Information Security Officer provides invaluable insights and guidance to ensure that information systems are secure from internal manipulation and external threats. The Chief Information Security Officer has functional capabilities under them through the security operations center, vulnerability management, and penetration testing to ensure that systems that are developed and rolled out are secure from any intrusion that could potentially lead to the unauthorized exposure of personal data.
Chief Information/Technology Officer	The Chief Information/Technology Officer is discharged for overseeing the development and deployment of AI systems within the organization, and working at the 1st line of defense, their presence can brief the committee and organizational stakeholders about the challenges and progress associated with AI systems.
Chief Legal Officer	Chief Legal Officers' insights are invaluable to ensure that Legal requirements, whether stemming from contractual or regulatory requirements, are being fulfilled. At the same time,

	various data privacy laws across the globe empower individuals with the right to action and the right to object to the automated processing of personal data. Thereby, it becomes pivotal to ensure that the organization is legally protected from such lawsuits.
	Additionally, data processing agreements are a consistent feature when it comes to data privacy. It is therefore vital to have a chief legal officer presence within the data privacy executive management committee.
Chief Strategy/Product Officer	Chief Strategy or Product Officers are often responsible for driving the business strategy and, therefore, have strategic initiatives dependent on personal data processing. Their presence in the oversight committee helps the organization balance innovation with the protection of individuals' rights and freedoms associated with personal data.

2.3.4 Privacy Risk Management & Impact Assessment Methodology

Most of the modern privacy regulatory instruments mandate or strongly recommend carrying out a privacy impact assessment specifically for high-risk processing activities.

EU GDPR enunciates under Article 35 the need to perform a data protection impact assessment. Similarly, the ISO 27701 PIMS also expresses the need to carry out privacy risk assessments.

Linkage between Privacy Impact Assessment & Privacy Risk Management Framework

One of the common puzzling questions that lurks in the minds of privacy professionals is around the linkage and connection between privacy impact assessment and privacy risk management.

Privacy Impact Assessment (PIA) is a tool to evaluate if the business processes, products, or services pose any privacy risks through the personal data.

Consider a scenario where an organization has to conduct a PIA without any governed and approved privacy taxonomy, impact, and likelihood levels, then how will such an organization is going to qualify/quantify privacy harms that may occur?

If PIA is not built on Privacy Risk Taxonomy and lexicon, which is encapsulated within the privacy risk management framework, then it's likely to be carried out in an ad hoc and ungoverned manner.

PIAs are tools to examine the risks/harms that may be caused to individuals by organizational pursuits. But for such tools (PIA) to function well, there has to be a defined, consistent, and approved mechanism that is blended within an organizational framework.

The privacy risk management framework defines the conditions, taxonomy, impact and likelihood scales, risk acceptance criteria, privacy risk appetite, and other key elements to ensure that the results of privacy impact assessments are reliable and consistent in identifying potential privacy harms to data subjects.

On the contrary, when PIAs are conducted in the absence of a privacy risk management framework or when PIAs are divorced from privacy risk management, then such impact assessment also gets disconnected from Enterprise Risk Management. In such cases, the senior management and the Board do not know about the organizational pursuits that are risky and counterintuitive to Privacy principles.

Privacy Impact Assessment Methodology

To initiate a privacy impact assessment, the data privacy team must understand the business objectives behind such personal data processing activities and the high-level flow of personal data between information systems, either within the organization or beyond.

The Data privacy function may have to perform privacy impact assessments on either of the two triggers, and the following tables propose the approaches that can be taken to conduct a PIA.

TRIGGERS FOR PIA	PROPOSED APPROACH
1. New Business pursuits or enhancements that require personal data processing.	Integrate PIA into a Privacy by Design to ensure privacy requirements are blended within various stages of the system's development lifecycle or project management cycle.
2. Existing business processes, products, and services that have already been processing personal data.	Conduct a stand-alone PIA since these business processes or services are likely to be carried out prior to the establishment of the data privacy function.

The below illustration reflects the high-level steps that need to be carried out within the Privacy impact assessment exercise.

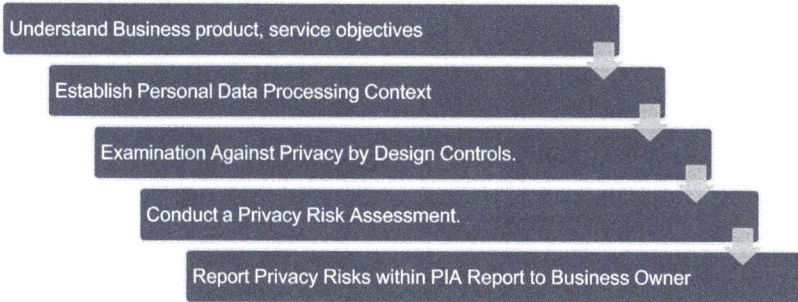

Understand Business product, service objectives

Establish Personal Data Processing Context

Examination Against Privacy by Design Controls.

Conduct a Privacy Risk Assessment.

Report Privacy Risks within PIA Report to Business Owner

Table 1 - PIA Section I

DESCRIPTION OF THE PRODUCT OR SERVICE		
This section must contain the high-level description of the product or service and the intended benefits that the business intends to reap out of such initiative.		
PERSONAL DATA PROCESSING CONTEXT		
Data Lifecycle Phase	**Areas**	**Business Owner Feedback**
Collection Phase	Source of Personal Data Collection	Options: • Data Subjects. • Third parties.
	Methods of Personal Data Collection.	Options: • Electronic Forms. • Papers. • APIs. • System integrations. • Cookies.

		• Other Methods.
Usage & Processing Phase	Description of the nature of processing to be conducted.	*These sections are preferred to be elaborate and free text.*
	Categories of personal data to be processed.	*These sections are preferred to be elaborate and free text.*
	Any personal data exchange with any third party.	*These sections are preferred to be elaborate and free text.*
	Any personal data exchange beyond jurisdiction.	*These sections are preferred to be elaborate and free text.*
Storage & Retention Phase	Geographic location of storage and retention	Country: City: Storage Model: On-prem/Cloud Cloud Provider: (if applicable) Name of any 3rd party: (if applicable)
	Data Retention Period (*Data Retention period must have a definite rationale in alignment with*	Express in terms of months or years.

	regulations, principles of proportionality, and data minimization)	
Disclosure Phase	Does personal data need to be transferred or disclosed to any external party within or outside the jurisdiction?	• Yes. • No
	Identify the country or region to which the PII needs to be transferred.	Example: • Europe • Germany
	Identify the entity receiving personal data.	XYZ Corporation.
Destruction Phase	Who is responsible for the destruction of data?	This section is preferred to be elaborate and free text.

Table 2 PIA Section II

PRIVACY BY DESIGN CONTROLS EXAMINATION		
REQUIREMENTS	**DESCRIPTION**	**Initial Assessment Response.**
1. Transparency & Lawful Purpose	Is there a lawful purpose defined for such processing? If yes, please mention the lawful purpose for processing.	
	Does your current privacy notice explain the purposes for which personal data will be collected in a clear, easy-to-understand language?	

	Is there a need to perform a Legitimate Interest Assessment? If yes, have you conducted such an assessment?	
2. Choice & Consent	Has consent (implicit/explicit) been solicited in accordance with principles of transparency, fairness, and informed choice?	
	Are consent records being maintained?	
	Does your service enable individuals to revoke consent?	
	Does your service cease PII processing immediately at the revocation of consent?	
3. Limit Data Collection & Processing	Have you ensured that all PII elements are necessary for processing?	
	Would the collected data be processed for any purpose other than what is expressed within the privacy notice?	
	Are all PII elements being collected in accordance with business, legal & regulatory requirements?	
4. Use, Retention & Destruction	Does your service prevent unauthorized access to PII?	
	Are access logs maintained for access to systems processing PII?	

	Have you identified the data retention period for PII processing? Mention duration and rationale?	
	Have you documented Data Flow Diagrams?	
	Does your service or product contain checkpoints or system logic to ensure that PII is systemically erased when no further processing is needed?	
	Does your service or product contain de-identification methods to reasonably prevent re-identification?	
	Does your service or product contain a garbage collection procedure to identify and delete relevant PII?	
	Ensure all PII is identified, inventoried, and classified.	
	Procedure to ensure that any unused temporary files are deleted have been identified?	
5. Data Subject Rights	Have you considered how Data subjects would be able to access their data for correction, review, and update purposes? Explain.	
	Have you considered how data subject access requests will be handled?	

6. Data Disclosure Limitation	Disclosure of personal data to third parties shall be restricted to the purposes provided for in the Privacy Notice.	
	Have you performed a 3rd party assessment (if applicable) on the parties that will be receiving personal data for the dispensation of services?	
7. Data Security	Have you established administrative and technical measures to protect Personal data from leakage, damage, loss, theft, misuse, modification, or unauthorized access?	
	Ensure erasure of data from third-party systems after processing needs have been fulfilled.	
8. Data Quality	Does your product or service contain checks and systemic logic to validate the accuracy, completeness, and timeliness of personal data?	
9. Data Transfer outside Jurisdiction	Have you identified the lawful purpose to transfer PII across different jurisdictions?	
	Identify if the destination jurisdiction falls under the adequacy list or if appropriate safeguards will be used to transfer personal data.	

Once the above examinations are performed, the privacy team must perform a thorough risk assessment using the privacy risk management framework. The approaching section expands upon the details associated with the establishment of privacy risk management frameworks and how it can be leveraged to conduct a Privacy risk assessment.

Privacy Risk Management Framework

Privacy Risk Management Framework is one of the most critical governing frameworks to be established for the privacy function to carry out privacy risk assessments. The entire edifice of the privacy impact assessments stands on the foundations of the privacy risk management framework.

The privacy risk management framework can be built around established risk management guidelines and principles, such as ISO31000 risk management guidelines and the ISO 27005 risk management framework, or the NIST privacy framework. This book highlights the approach that can be used to establish a Privacy risk management framework in line with ISO standards. Therefore organizations opting to adopt the NIST Privacy Framework may need to make slight adjustments in establishing and implementing a privacy risk management framework.

ISO 27701 Privacy information management system does not exhort for adoption of any specific risk management methodology to be adopted by the organization, and it leaves it to the discretion of the organization to determine the best methodology in accordance with their business nature, objectives, and operational activities.

The Privacy Risk Management framework enables the Privacy functional unit to qualify/quantify harms that may occur to the data subjects because of the personal data processing activities. Therefore, a risk management framework must be built to identify, analyze, assess, and act upon such risks.

The Privacy risk management framework must be integrated with the Enterprise Risk Management framework to ensure that privacy risks that are above the organizational risk appetite are duly reported to the board of directors. This significantly helps in putting privacy in the spotlight within the organization's senior management and the board of directors.

A conventional risk management framework entails the stages exhibited in the next figure, which can be adopted to establish a privacy risk management framework.

In the same breadth, the data privacy function must work with the Enterprise Risk Management function to ensure that the organization Risk Appetit e statements capture the privacy risk appetite statements and their thresholds.

For all risks identified, the risk owner must be identified and held accountable for the risk treatment; however, a challenge often pops up within the organizations when the risk owners are dependent on the control owners to implement a control associated with a specific risk treatment plan.

We will now unpack the various stages of the risk management below.

- **Context Establishment.**

The first step in the establishment of privacy risk management is to establish the context within which the privacy risks will be examined and responded. The stage must enunciate the factors at the Global and national level, industry level, and the organizational level that can impact the organization. Risk context provides a structured method to identify the internal and external variables that may influence personal data protection.

In some organizations, the risk context is encapsulated along with the Enterprise Risk Management. Therefore, one must work with ERM to ensure that the risk context captures the privacy landscape that may affect the organization.

Privacy risks are influenced by factors that could be internal or external, and they could be either within or beyond organizational control. Emerging technologies like AI, facial recognition, Internet of Things, blockchain, etc., and their adoption by the organization leave an impact on the privacy risk landscape.

Additionally, cybersecurity threats associated with ransomware, data leakage add to the privacy risk landscape.

- **Global & National Level**

The risk context must highlight the developments taking place at the global and national levels that have intersections with personal data protection and have a likelihood of impacting organizational business pursuits.

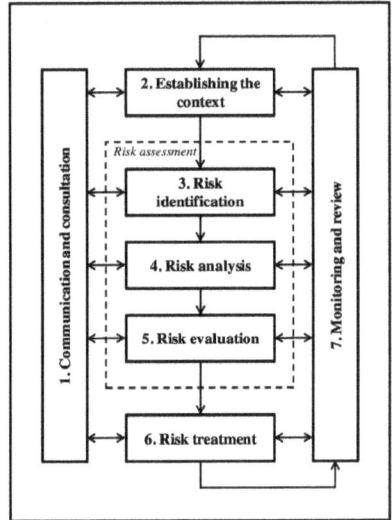

It could be related to the development of new privacy laws and regulations at international and national levels, which may affect the organization, or it could also be a change of penalty structures within existing laws that can impact the organization.

- **Industry or Sector Level**

Industries and sectors have their own unique risk portfolio, as each industry faces different privacy concerns depending on how sensitive they are to the protection of personal data and because of the ramifications associated with the adverse impact. The data privacy function must identify the sector and industry in which it operates and must record the context accordingly. Below are the examples that can be beneficial to establish the privacy risk context with respect to the industry or sector.

- *Healthcare/Medical Sector*

The personal data processed in the industry or sector is largely sensitive in nature, ranging from medical records, genetic information, and health conditions. Such data landscape therefore attracts more attention from the regulators, which is expressed in the form of sector-specific regulations like HIPAA, etc.

Such personal data is only considered a hot cake for malicious actors, and thereby any personal data breaches of such data may lead to identity theft, fraud, extortion, blackmailing, or insurance exploitation. The risk context must factor in that conventional healthcare regulations advocate and protect patient rights over their health data, often requiring explicit consent mechanisms and robust access management.

- *Banking & Financial Services Sector*

The latitude of personal data processed in this industry makes it a prime target for fraudsters and cybercriminals. For example, various regulations require the stringent application of information security controls to protect such data because the privacy of individuals may become a casualty due to poor information security hygiene.

The risk context must factor in that regulations that advocate stringent transaction validations and protection to prevent scenarios related to fraud, sponsoring criminal and terror activities or money laundering.

- *Government and Public Sector*

The public or the government entities are often collecting, processing, or handling massive amounts of personal data, which may be collected for national security purposes and may fall under mass surveillance and citizen profiling categories. The government entity must examine the latitude of personal data being processed by them and the accountability requirements imposed by the privacy laws or their relevant ministries.

Such entities are often required to ensure strong personal data protection mechanisms to prevent any outreach and unauthorized exposure or processing of personal data. Additionally, there are requirements related to data sovereignty and localization where the government and public entities are required to store and process data within the geographical boundaries of the country.

- **Organizational Level**

The privacy risk context may encapsulate mission-critical and other major processes linked to personal data processing and their impact on stakeholders like consumers, employees, and business partners etc., along with the expectations of the individuals/data subjects around transparency and their control over their data.

It is beneficial to put on record the potential pitfalls of non-compliance related to privacy regulations and personal data breaches, which could result in penalties, fines, and reputational damage to the organization.

While the penalties and fines may be easier to quantify, the erosion of customer trust and loyalty is often difficult to quantify

Identify Risk Appetite, Risk Evaluation Criteria, and Risk Acceptance Criteria.

The **Privacy risk appetite statements** must be clearly captured within the risk context and reported to the Enterprise risk management and the Chief Risk Officer if they cross certain thresholds. This requires closer collaboration with the enterprise risk management function as there are specific mandates and reporting obligations upon the Enterprise risk management function and the chief risk officer.

The **Risk Evaluation criteria** help to assess and compare risks. It determines risk severity and informs Risk Acceptance about whether the risk can be accepted or requires further action.

The risk evaluation criteria express how the organization will act on the identified risks based on their severity levels. Below is an illustration of the risk evaluation criteria that the organizations can adopt.

RISK LEVELS	EVALUATION CRITERIA
CRITICAL	Urgent Action must be taken.
MAJOR	Reduce the risk to bring it within the acceptable levels.

MODERATE	Reduce risk considering the cost of prevention compared to a reduction in risk.
LOW	No further reduction is needed.

Risk Acceptance Criteria defines the conditions under which a risk is considered acceptable or tolerable. It determines the severity of risks an organization is willing to accept without further mitigation. Risk acceptance criteria act as a threshold, which means that if risk severity is exceeded, then it must be treated through specific risk response mechanisms.

Below is an illustration of the risk acceptance criteria that can be adopted by the organizations.

RISK LEVELS	ACCEPTANCE CRITERIA
CRITICAL	• Unacceptable Risk. Risk Treatment plans must be devised and implemented immediately. • Treatment plans need to be implemented, investigated, and monitored.
MAJOR	• Can be accepted provided that continual monitoring is in place. • Treatment plans need to be implemented, investigated, and monitored.
MODERATE	• Can be accepted with documented justification.
LOW	• Can be accepted without documented justification.

- **Impact Severity: Evaluate potential harm (e.g., financial loss, identity theft, reputational damage).**
- **Likelihood of Occurrence: Assess how probable a privacy breach or non-compliance incident is.**
- **Risk Appetite and Escalation: Determine acceptable risk thresholds and required mitigation actions.**

- **Risk Assessment Phase**

The Privacy risk management framework must capture activities that will be performed within the risk assessment phase. The risk assessment phase consists of **Risk Identification, Risk Analysis,** and **Risk Evaluation** activities as depicted in the Figure above.

- **Risk Identification.**

This is the first activity in the Privacy Risk Assessment where potential privacy risks are identified with regard to personal data processing. The risk identification activity starts with the identification of a risk scenario that needs to be examined. Below is a table of the privacy risk library that you can leverage within your organizational privacy risk management framework.

Once the privacy risk scenario has been identified, then the following information must be captured into your risk register in a sequential manner, so that your privacy risk management framework must have a taxonomy developed for these elements.

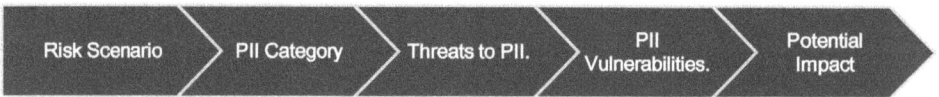

Risk Scenario | PII Category | Threats to PII. | PII Vulnerabilities. | Potential Impact

Figure 8 Risk Identification Steps

Table 3 - Non-Exhaustive Privacy Risks Library

RISK LIBRARY	
RISK SCENARIOS	**DESCRIPTION**
1. Unauthorized Collection & Processing	Relates to scenarios when any personal data is collected and processed without any identified lawful purpose. This includes any processing activities that may be performed even by internal departments for investigations, research, or analytical purposes.
2. Transparency & Fairness Risk	Relates to scenarios when individuals are not served a privacy notice or are not transparently explained the mechanisms for personal data processing.

3. Inappropriate Consent Solicitation	Relates to scenarios when consent is a lawful purpose of processing, but consent is not being obtained, or its records are not being stored.
4. Automated Decision-Making Bias	Relates to scenarios when various PII elements are aggregated together for automated decision making that can have a legal and significant impact on the rights and freedoms of the individuals.
5. Undue retention of personal data.	Relates to scenarios when personal data is retained within the organization regardless of the environment beyond its lawful retention period.
6. Failure to Securely Dispose of Personal Data	Relates to scenarios when personal data is not disposed of securely at the end of the data retention period.
7. Insecure Storage and Processing of Personal Data.	Relates to scenarios when personal data is stored and processed using insecure means, offering inadequate protection and posing a threat to the data.
8. Unauthorized access to personal data.	Relates to scenarios when personal data is likely to become a casualty because of access granted to unauthorized individuals.
9. Third-Party Vendor Risks	Relates to scenarios when personal data is likely to be exchanged with third parties and vendors that lack adequate privacy protection or a program within their organization.
10. Cross-Border Data Transfer Compliance Issues	Relates to scenarios when personal data is transferred to a jurisdiction that does not offer safeguards and protections to the personal data.
11. Failure to Dispense Data Subject Requests	Relates to the organizational inability to dispense the rights of the data subjects efficiently and judiciously.

Below is a non-exhaustive list of personal data identifiers that the organization may use to carry out their personal data processing activities.

Table 4 Non-Exhaustive List of PII Categories

PII CATEGORY
1. Name
2. Credit Card Statement
3. Financial Profile
4. Conviction reports for LEA or legal authorities.
5. Biometric Information.
6. Racial or Ethnic Information
7. Passport ID/National ID
8. Date of Birth
9. Location Information
10. Bank Account.
11. Communication Channel Information (Email, Contact #)

Below is a non-exhaustive list of threats to personal data identifiers that the organization may use to identify potential threats.

Table 5 - Non-Exhaustive List of Threats to PII

THREATS TO PERSONAL DATA IDENTIFIERS	
PII THREATS TAXONOMY	DESCRIPTION
Unlawful collection	• Collecting disproportionate personal data and violating principles of proportionality. • Collection of PII through coercive, covert, or deceptive means.

	• Opaque Consent Mechanisms using dark patterns to trick data subjects or violate the requirement for freely given and informed exercise of choice.
Personal Data Breach	Unauthorized access, alteration, loss of availability, or disclosure of personal data.
Data Correlation and Re-Identification	• Linking distinct data identifiers to identify individuals. • Generating new personal data by inference profiling and behavioral analytics.
Ransomware & Spyware	*Malicious software used to attack data availability and confidentiality through encryption of content stored on either of the following:* • *Information systems.* • *Storages.*
User Impersonation	*Scenario leading to disclosure of personal information such as user ID, password, National IDs, Passport ID, etc., and usage of such information for authentication purposes.*

Reference: ETSI TR 103 304 - CYBER; Personally Identifiable Information (PII) Protection in mobile and cloud services

Below is a non-exhaustive list of vulnerabilities that may affect personal data and resultantly cause privacy risks to the individuals.

Table 6 Non-Exhaustive list of PII Vulnerabilities

PII VULNERABILITIES TAXONOMY
Inadequate Credentials and Key Management
Lack of Information Classification or labelling.
Poor Identification & Authentication Mechanism
Improper allocation of Access Rights
Lack of Access Control

Lack of clean desks and clear screen policy
Lack of Policy, Process, Procedure.

Once the Privacy risk scenario has been selected and the associated threat and its vulnerability have been identified within the risk register, you must proceed with identification the potential impact. It's pivotal to understand that in privacy risk assessment, we must determine the impact on the rights, interests, and freedoms of the individuals and not the organizations. It is to be noted that often one impact feeds the other impact. Therefore, the privacy professionals must exercise diligence in identifying the primary impact in the risk assessment phase.

Below is a non-exhaustive list of potential impacts that may affect personal data and resultantly cause privacy risks to the individuals. The list below of potential impacts can be used to assess the fundamental rights damage to the individuals.

POTENTIAL IMPACT ON DATA SUBJECTS	
POTENTIAL IMPACT TAXONOMY	**EXAMPLES**
Financial Impact	• Financial fraud and loss due to credential or identity theft. • Failure to avail of insurance or government benefits. • Financial Extortion where personal data is exploited to seek a ransom from individuals
Physical & Psychological Impact	• Exposure of address, real-time location tracking impacts the physical well-being of an individual. • Emotional Distress in the form of Anxiety, fear, or trauma due to exposure to personal data. • Self-censorship causes individuals to repress their feelings and concerns. • Cyber-bullying, harassment, and discrimination due to exposure of personal details, including sensitive personal

	data attributes or attributes that are often used to discriminate against individuals.
Reputational & Legal Damage	• Exposure of Private Life Details such as personal photos, messages, or logs of online activities, such as consumption of social media content, etc. • Employment and legal ramifications due to past actions, affiliations, or opinions. • Unauthorized use of personal data to create false narratives about an individual. • False attributions and criminal allegations.

• **Risk Analysis.**

The privacy risk management framework must capture the steps that will be involved in the Risk analysis phase. Organizations may perform qualitative or quantitative analysis depending on their organizational compulsions. Various risk analysis techniques exist; however, they are beyond the scope of discussion within this book.

During the risk analysis, the following steps must be performed.

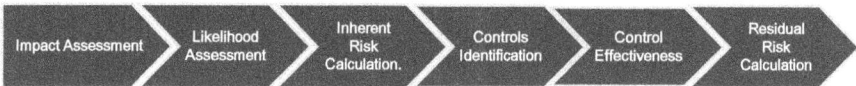

Figure 9 Risk Analysis Steps

Once the potential impacts are identified during the Risk identification, it is imperative to assess the consequences/impacts on the individuals. For example, the data privacy function must work with the enterprise risk management function to determine the matrix structure that the ERM is following so that Privacy impact, likelihood, and risk severity scale are aligned with Enterprise risk management.

For example, if the ERM is following a 5 x 5 (Impact x Likelihood), 4 x 5 (Impact x Likelihood), or 3x3 (Impact x Likelihood), then the Privacy risk management framework must align itself with a similar matrix.

Below is an illustration that exemplifies the impact assessment scale that can be adopted by the organizations.

LEVEL	QUALITATIVE SCALE	CONSEQUENCES/IMPACT
1	INSIGNIFICANT	The impact caused to the individuals will be negligible.
2	MINOR	The impact caused to individuals will be limited without causing any inconvenience.
3	MEDIUM	The impact caused to individuals will be limited, causing inconveniences.
4	MAJOR	The impact caused to individuals will be significant, causing a serious impact.
5	CRITICAL	The impact caused to individuals will be significant and may cause irreversible consequences.

Below is an illustration that exemplifies the likelihood assessment scale that can be adopted by the organizations.

LEVEL	QUALITATIVE SCALE	LIKELIHOOD
0	VERY RARE	The event never occurred before and is not expected to occur under normal circumstances.
1	RARE	The event occurred only in rare cases due to the presence of specific vulnerabilities.
2	POSSIBLE	The event has a moderate probability of occurrence.
3	VERY PROSSIBLE	The event has a significant probability of occurrence.
4	COMMON	The event is extremely probable to occur frequently.

The privacy management framework must be able to compute the values of the impact scale and likelihood scale to determine the level of various privacy risk scenarios identified.

Below is an example of how risk levels can be computed from impact and likelihood scales. The risk assessment matrix below can be used to determine the inherent risks.

LIKELIHOOD	RISK ASSESSMENT MATRIX				
COMMON (5)	5	10	15	20	25
VERY POSSIBLE (4)	4	8	12	16	20
POSSIBLE (3)	3	6	9	12	15
RARE (2)	2	4	6	8	10
VERY RARE (1)	1	2	3	4	5

IMPACT	INSIGNIFICANT (1)	MINOR (2)	MEDIUM (3)	MAJOR (4)	CRITICAL (5)

RISK LEVELS	RISK SCORE RANGE
CRITICAL	25
MAJOR	15—20
MODERATE	9—12
LOW	1—8

The privacy risk management framework and the risk register must capture the existing controls to handle the risk scenario, and all the identified controls must also be rated for their effectiveness.

The following Control effectiveness table is an illustration that the organizations can use to gauge the effectiveness of privacy controls.

CONTROL RATING	DESCRIPTION
STRONG & RESILIENT	Controls are well-designed, planned, and consistently implemented, leaving little to no residue. Controls are periodically tested for their consistency and resilience. Controls are aligned with best practices and compliance obligations.
MODERATE	Controls are adequate and functional, but may require some adjustments with respect to certain risk scenarios. Controls may require minor enhancements or consistent application to ensure personal data protection.
INEFFECTIVE AND WEAK	Controls exist but are poorly designed, configured, or operated, making them ineffective.
NON-EXISTENT	Controls are absent or not relevant to the risk.

Taking the inherent risks and control assessment into view, the data privacy unit must calculate the residual risk using the same impact and likelihood scales.

- **Risk Evaluation**

The conclusion of the risk analysis phase will provide an input to risk evaluation to determine which risk needs to be treated and the most appropriate risk treatment strategy and methods.

Once done, the Risk Evaluation will be the process of comparing the results of risk analysis with risk criteria to determine whether the risk and/or its impact is acceptable based on the guidance and Risk Acceptance criteria stipulated within the Context Establishment phase.

Risk Evaluation will help in further curating the Risk Register and developing a list of prioritized risks in accordance with Risk Evaluation Criteria.

The prioritized risks are those that are above the Enterprise risk acceptable range and require a risk treatment plan.

- **Risk Treatment.**

Organizations have four conventional approaches towards Risk Treatment, which are illustrated below.

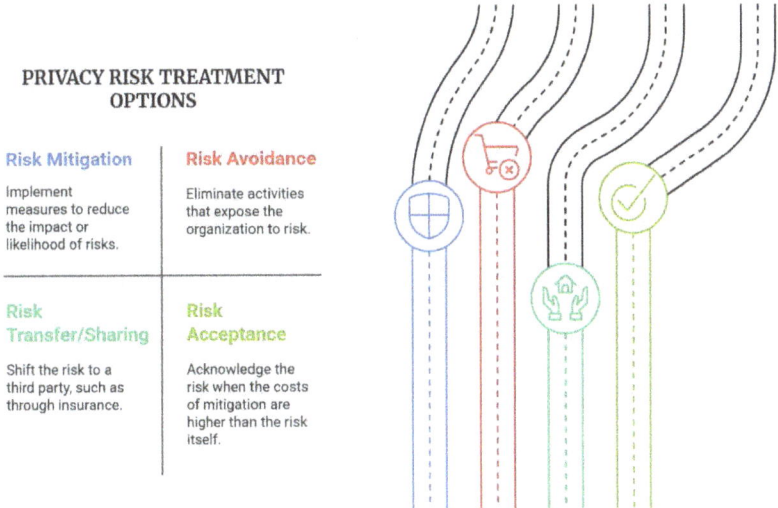

Figure 10 - Privacy Risk Treatment Options

For each risk identified and analyzed within the privacy risk register, there must be one of the following risk treatment options that must be exercised.

PRIVACY RISK TREATMENT OPTIONS	
RISK MITIGATION	**RISK ACCEPTANCE**
• Reduce risk by applying proportionate privacy controls. ○ *Assess the cost of implementing the Privacy controls* ○ *Assess the feasibility of implementing the Privacy controls.*	Accepting Privacy risks should include: The consideration of predefined limits for levels of privacy risk. The approval and sign-off by the business owner, ensuring that: ○ *The accepted privacy risk is within the risk appetite and is reported to the Risk Committee.* ○ *The accepted privacy risk does not contradict privacy regulations.*
RISK AVOIDANCE	**RISK TRANSFER/SHARING**
• Involves a decision by a business owner to cancel or postpone a particular activity or project that introduces an unacceptable privacy risk.	Transferring or sharing the Privacy risks should involve sharing the privacy risks with relevant (internal or external) service providers.

- **Risk Communication, Reporting, and Monitoring.**

The privacy risk management framework must enlist the requirements for communication, reporting, and monitoring of privacy risks to various stakeholders. Below considerations are recommended to be included within the privacy risk management framework.

- Once the privacy risk assessment exercise is completed, then the privacy impact assessment and risk register must be sent to the business owner for confirmation of results, identified risks, risk treatment plan, and the timeframe to treat the risks. This is pivotal for effective stakeholder engagement and timely mitigation of privacy risks.
- Privacy Risk Landscape must be communicated and reported to the Privacy oversight committee, ensuring that all risks are treated within the given timeline.

- The committee must be apprised of any risks that are overdue and above the risk appetite of the organization.
- Risk above the risk appetite must be communicated to the Enterprise Risk Management function so that they are reported to the Chief Risk Officer, CEO, and the Board in an appropriate timeframe for remediation.
- The risk owners must also be exhorted to monitor the implementation of the risk treatment plan to ensure that the risks are treated timely. If there are any expected delays, then the privacy unit must be duly informed.

The privacy risk management framework should also include a process for assessing any third parties involved in handling personal data. Since many organizations already have an enterprise-wide third-party or vendor risk management system, it is important for the privacy team to integrate their specific requirements into this system. This ensures that privacy-related risks associated with third parties are properly evaluated. The questionnaire below can be used to gauge the operational effectiveness of the 3rd party involved in personal data processing.

AREAS	THIRD PARTY/VENDOR ASSESSMENT CRITERIA	Response
Data Privacy Policies & Procedures	Do you have policies and procedures to ensure the protection of personal data?	
	Do you have any personal data protection strategy or program in place?	
	Do you have an appointed Data Protection Officer?	
	Do you comply or adhere to any privacy laws, standards, or best practices?	
Jurisdiction	List all the geographical locations in which the personal data will be processed.	
	Will you be transferring the personal data to some other parties in additional jurisdictions?	
	Will you be collecting any personal data on our behalf?	

	Do you ensure that you collect personal data only for the purposes identified in the notices?	
	Do you have access controls in place to ensure personal data is limited to business purposes?	
	Do you conduct a Privacy impact assessment exercise?	
Personal Data Processing & Operations	Does your staff access the personal data hosted on your servers from a geographical location beyond your jurisdiction? If "yes," then please explain how the access control is exercised.	
	Is there any third party/vendor that is being used for this agreement, including a cloud service provider? If yes, then please provide sufficient details.	
	Do you have an active and functioning Data Retention & Disposal procedure in place?	
	Do you have a system in place to detect any personal data breaches? If yes, please describe the mechanism to detect and report such breaches.	

The business owners can be provided with the above questionnaire to be relayed to third parties for their response submission. Once the third parties and the vendors submit their responses, the data privacy function must perform an assessment using the data collected.

The Privacy risk register must also capture all the privacy risks associated with third-party or vendor.

Placing Hooks for PIAs in Organizational Processes

The data privacy functional unit must ensure that they have placed the hooks within the organizational processes that will trigger the business units to get PIAs performed. The following table enlists the key touch points for placing hooks and triggers for Privacy Impact Assessment.

ORGANIZATIONAL PROCESS	EXPLANATION
Product/Systems' Development Lifecycle	o PIAs are a component of the Privacy by Design framework. o PIAs are to be performed once the initial product or service design is prepared. Planning and Design details equip privacy teams to perform a thorough privacy impact assessment.
Third parties or Vendor Onboarding	o Organizations have their enterprise third-party or vendor risk assessment in which privacy and security assessments can be embedded.
IT Enhancements or System Upgrades affecting Personal Data processing.	o Applicable in cases when a technological shift or infrastructure change, or enhancement affects the manner in which personal data is being processed. Example: Cloud migrations
Mergers, Acquisitions & Divestitures.	o Conduct PIAs for due diligence on data handling practices of acquired entities. o Assess cross-border data flows and compliance with data privacy laws and regulations.

2.3.5 Privacy Compliance Framework

The Privacy Compliance Framework is another critical component to ensure effective Privacy governance. It is one of the key responsibilities of the data privacy function to establish a Unified Privacy Compliance framework that encompasses all the regulatory and conformity instruments that the organization must adhere to.

As it was expressed earlier, the privacy regulatory instruments and the international best practices or standards are a key input to the development of the Data Privacy Program. The edifice of the Data Privacy program strongly rests on the privacy regulatory and conformity requirements.

However, the value of a unified privacy compliance framework lives beyond the complete execution of the Data Privacy program, considering that a program has a specific life with objectives to be achieved in a certain time. In contrast, the unified privacy compliance framework enables the organization to ensure that organization continues to follow the personal data protection principles and requirements on a continuous basis.

- **Stakeholder Management & Guidance for Privacy Compliance**

When embarking on establishing a unified privacy framework, it is advisable to collaborate with your Compliance department to ensure that the Unified Privacy Compliance framework entails all the necessary instruments with tangents to personal data protection. Otherwise, it may result in failure to develop a comprehensive compliance roadmap.

The unified privacy compliance framework must clearly distinguish which instruments require regulatory compliance and which ones require conformity.

While the instruments for privacy regulatory compliance and international best practices are both essential to uphold personal data protection principles and ethical use of personal data, it is important to distinguish between the two because the ramifications for both kinds of instruments vary in nature. The senior management must be apprised of the consequences associated with non-compliance and non-conformity.

Privacy Regulatory Compliance Instruments

Instruments that take the form of privacy laws, regulations, and legal obligations are considered regulatory compliance instruments. They are established by the government or the regulatory authorities empowered by the government. The creation of privacy laws and regulations requires deeper deliberations among the stakeholders at the national or, often, at the regional level to ensure cohesion in understanding.

Failure to comply with this kind of instrument may lead to penalties, fines, or license revocations as well. Some privacy regulations often empower individuals to seek the right to action against organizations. Therefore, regulatory compliance is often non-negotiable to the business.

2. Conformance

Conformance is the organization's voluntary adherence to international or industry standards, best practices, or frameworks. Such instruments are not legally binding but support the organization to adopt personal data protection principles, which are embodied within those standards, best practices, guidelines, or frameworks.

The voluntary adherence to such international or industry standards, best practices, or frameworks helps the organization to foster trust in their products and services and largely helps them gain a competitive advantage over their competitors.

The non-conformity with such instruments does not lead to regulatory fines or penalties. Still, it can erode the consumer trust in the products and services of your organization.

The below table provides a comparative view between the two instruments.

Areas	Regulatory Compliance Instruments	Conformity Instruments
Source	Imposed by government or regulatory authorities in the form of laws and regulations. - Obligatory in Nature	Established by independent bodies or regulatory bodies. - Voluntary (based on industry best practices)
Enforcement	Regulatory & Enforcement authorities	Industry bodies (ISO, NIST, CIS)
Flexibility	Firm & Assertive, requiring organizations to follow prescribed controls.	Flexible, allowing organizations to choose standards based on relevance and readiness.
Consequences of non-adherence	Fines, lawsuits, penalties, and right of actions.	Erosion of consumer trust.
Examples (Non-exhaustive)	• GDPR. • CCPA. • HIPAA.	• ISO 27701 PIMS. • NIST Privacy Framework. • ISO 29134.

Below are the non-exhaustive lists of standards and regulations that an organization may choose or be obligated to adhere to, depending on the jurisdiction and the sector in which the organization operates.

North America		
United States	○	California Consumer Privacy Act (CCPA) (2018) / California Privacy Rights Act (CPRA) (2023).
	○	Children's Online Privacy Protection Act (COPPA) (1998)
	○	Federal Trade Commission Act (FTC Act) Section 5 (Unfair and Deceptive Practices)
	○	State-Specific Privacy Laws
CANADA	○	**Personal Information Protection and Electronic Documents Act (PIPEDA)** (2000)
	○	**Provincial Privacy Laws** (e.g., Quebec Law 25, BC PIPA, Alberta PIPA)
EUROPE		
European Union	○	General Data Protection Regulation (GDPR) (2016, effective 2018)
	○	Digital Services Act (DSA)
UK	○	**UK GDPR** (Post-Brexit adaptation of GDPR)
SOUTH AMERICA		
BRAZIL	○	Lei Geral de Proteção de Dados (LGPD)
MIDDLE EAST		
UNITED ARAB EMIRATES	○	Dubai International Financial Centre (DIFC) Data Protection Law
	○	Abu Dhabi Global Market (ADGM) Data Protection Regulation
SAUDI ARABIA	○	Personal Data Protection Law (PDPL)
QATAR	○	**Personal Data Protection Law**

ASIA-PACIFIC	
CHINA	○ Personal Information Protection Law (PIPL) ○ Data Security Law.
INDIA	○ Digital Personal Data Protection Act (DPDP Act)
SINGAPORE	○ Personal Data Protection Act (PDPA)

Industry-Specific Privacy Regulations

Financial Services			
Regulation	**Jurisdiction**	**Sector**	**Description**
Gramm-Leach-Bliley Act (GLBA)	USA	Financial Services	Requires financial institutions to protect customer data.
Sarbanes-Oxley Act (SOX)	USA	Financial Services	Imposes requirements for corporate governance and data privacy.
Payment Card Industry Data Security Standard (PCI DSS)	Global	Financial Services	Security standard for handling credit card data.
Health Insurance Portability and Accountability Act (HIPAA)	**USA**	Health Sector	Protects personal health information (PHI).
HITECH Act	**USA**	Health Sector	Expands HIPAA security and enforcement.

Telecommunications & Media			
Regulation	**Jurisdiction**	**Sector**	**Description**
ePrivacy Directive (Cookie Law)	EU	Telecom & Digital Services	Regulates cookies, spam, and online tracking.
Federal Communications Commission (FCC) Privacy Rules	USA	Telecom	Regulates telecom companies' handling of customer data.

International Standards, Best Practices & Benchmarks		
Standard	**Published By**	**Description**
ISO/IEC 27701	ISO (International Organization for Standardization)	Built and extended upon ISO 27001 for Privacy Information Management System.
ISO/IEC 27001	ISO (International Organization for Standardization)	Information Security Management System (ISMS) standard.
ISO/IEC 27018	ISO (International Organization for Standardization)	Code of practice for cloud privacy.
NIST Privacy Framework	NIST (National Institute of Standards and Technology, USA)	Guidelines for risk-based privacy management.
CIS Critical Security Controls	Center for Internet Security (CIS)	Best practices for securing data and systems.

Ethical & Consumer-Centric Privacy Standards		
Standard	Published By	Description
Fair Information Practice Principles (FIPPs)	OECD & FTC	Foundation for privacy laws worldwide.
APEC Privacy Framework	APEC (Asia-Pacific Economic Cooperation)	Business-friendly privacy guidelines for Asia-Pacific countries.

- **Compliance Assessment Frequency**

The Unified Privacy Compliance framework must entail the frequency at which the data privacy functional unit will assess the adherence to and conformity with privacy regulatory instruments and standards.

While the frequency of such assessment may significantly depend upon the regulatory obligations, the nature of the business, size of the organization and its geographic spread, however it is advisable to conduct the privacy compliance assessments at least once a year or on a quarterly basis if there is higher sensitivity attached to the business processes or when the compliance initiatives are still underway.

When the data privacy functional unit is performing privacy compliance assessments, it is essential to keep track of all evidence attached to all obligations encapsulated within the regulations and the standards. The evidence is beneficial in case of any audits being conducted vis-à-vis personal data protection and helps to demonstrate the maturity of the data privacy function. When the data privacy functional unit has gathered and produced periodic Privacy compliance assessment reports, ensuring that all underlying evidence is gathered and stored, it fosters trust in the minds of the auditors.

- **Privacy Compliance Reporting & Accountability**

Once the compliance assessments are performed, they must be reported to the relevant oversight committees at the management and Board of Directors level.

This helps the management and board of directors understand the obligations related to personal data protection. Additionally, any gaps in adherence to the regulatory instruments or standards must carry a corrective action plan with timelines and owners to ensure that such requirements are implemented.

It is also beneficial to multi-cast the privacy compliance assessment report to stakeholders illustrated below to keep them informed about the privacy compliance landscape, challenges, reasons behind non-compliance or non-conformity, and the actions that must be taken to bridge the gaps.

Proposed Audience of Privacy Compliance Assessment Report

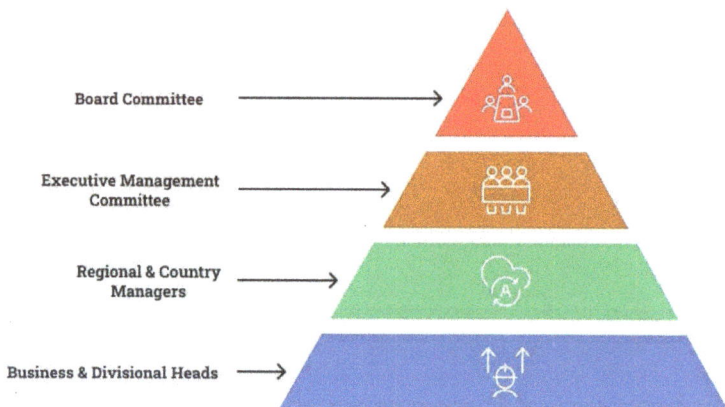

Figure 11 *Proposed Audience of Privacy Compliance Assessment Report*

Considerations for Privacy Compliance Assessment Report Structure

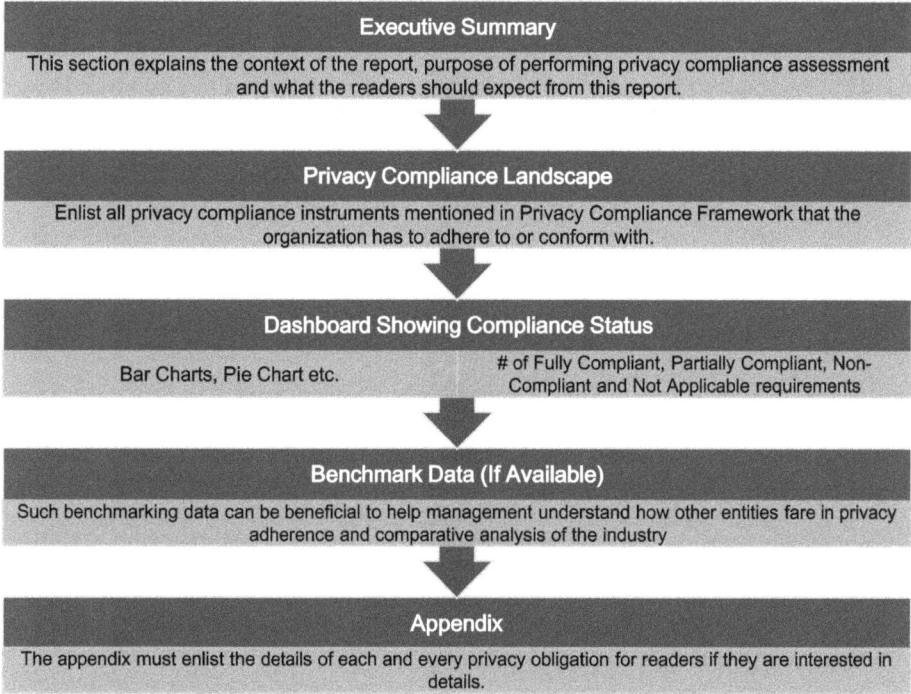

Executive Summary
This section explains the context of the report, purpose of performing privacy compliance assessment and what the readers should expect from this report.

Privacy Compliance Landscape
Enlist all privacy compliance instruments mentioned in Privacy Compliance Framework that the organization has to adhere to or conform with.

Dashboard Showing Compliance Status	
Bar Charts, Pie Chart etc.	# of Fully Compliant, Partially Compliant, Non-Compliant and Not Applicable requirements

Benchmark Data (If Available)
Such benchmarking data can be beneficial to help management understand how other entities fare in privacy adherence and comparative analysis of the industry

Appendix
The appendix must enlist the details of each and every privacy obligation for readers if they are interested in details.

The DPOs can benefit from adopting the Privacy compliance assessment report structure shown below.

Below is an illustration of the Privacy obligation card to capture the compliance details for each control/obligation within the privacy compliance instrument.

PRIVACY CONTROL/OBLIGATION COMPLIANCE CARD			
Control Description		Compliance Status	
Current Approach to Implementation			
Evidence List		Corrective Action Plan	

		(In case of Non-compliant or Partially Compliant)	
		Expected Compliance Date/Deadline	

2.3.6 Privacy Notice & Data Subject Rights Framework.

Establishing Privacy notices and dispensing them to the individuals is essential to uphold the principle of Openness, Transparency & Notice, which was discussed earlier in the Personal data protection principles section. The organization may have to serve various kinds of privacy notices depending on the nature of personal data processing activities undertaken. It may become too cumbersome for the DPO to encapsulate the details of all the personal data processing activities within a single privacy notice.

It is therefore recommended that an organization adopt a separate privacy notice for its business products and services, candidates (potential job seekers), existing employees, or vendors, and a cookie notice.

The fundamentals to establish a privacy notice will always remain the same, with certain adjustments to be accounted for each kind of privacy notice.

Significance of Privacy Notice from Legal and Compliance Standpoint

A privacy notice is a tool to ensure transparency around the personal data processing activities pursued by the organization. The Privacy notice is a notice to be provided to data subjects who could be your employees, vendors, visitors, or consumers of your products and services.

From a data subject's perspective, it enables them to understand how and why an organization is collecting and processing personal data and the underlying legal basis for each personal data processing activity. The objective behind such dispensation is to hold organizations accountable and open in front of the data subjects and to enable the data subjects to question the organizational pursuits with regard to personal data processing.

From an organizational perspective, the dispensation of the privacy notice is also expressed as a right to be informed within the data subject rights of various privacy regulations. When an organization issues a privacy notice, it is fulfilling its legal and compliance obligations. It is also to be kept in view that a privacy notice is an expression of commitment to the data subjects.

Therefore, an organization must abide by its statements within the privacy notice. When an organization deviates from what is expressed in the privacy notice, it enables the data subject to question the personal data processing activities and seek a remedy in the competent courts within the jurisdiction.

It is critically important that privacy notices are developed and maintained with proper stakeholders' input and approval to ensure that the privacy notices do not raise compliance risks.

Establishing a Privacy Notice Development & Maintenance Mechanism

The Data Privacy unit must establish a mechanism through which the privacy notices will be developed at broadcast to the data subjects through appropriate channels and touchpoints.

This requires establishing a procedural mechanism where various organizational stakeholders work with the Privacy function to draft and finalize the privacy notice on a periodic basis.

Privacy notices must be reviewed by the relevant business unit heads or chief officers whose teams participated in the development and review of the privacy notice. Once the privacy notices have been through a collaborative stakeholder arrangement, then they must be approved by the competent authority within the organization. The Delegate of Authority document, which is often maintained by the corporate governance, must encapsulate the approving authority of the privacy notices.

Common stakeholders that can be beneficial in the development and review of the Privacy Notice are below. It is important to note that the organizational dynamics will vary from one organization to another. In this regard, the list below is only meant to offer guidance and not to be taken as an obligation:

STAKEHOLDER	RATIONALE
Legal Department	Can support in validating the legal requirements for personal data processing and transfer. The legal department can be beneficial in providing a nuanced understanding of privacy laws.

Data Protection Officer (Data Privacy)	DPO is a subject matter expert, understanding the legal and compliance obligations associated with establishing and dispensing a privacy notice.
Business Departments	This may include different business departments or units that are responsible for collecting and processing personal data, including Marketing, sales, product management, HR, finance, etc.
Compliance Department	The Compliance department is essential to provide support and clarification in case of any conflicts with regards to compliance obligations related to the privacy notice. Their support can be handy in case there occurs a conflict arises between stakeholders with regard to understanding compliance requirements.
Data Management, Information Security, etc.	Teams like information security and data management can provide valuable support to highlight aspects related to data security and data retention measures taken by the organization.

Privacy Notice: Common Elements

There are numerous guidelines and recommendations that are put forward by the regulatory bodies and other advisory bodies on the structure of the privacy notice. This section avoids reinforcing the guidelines that are already available. Below are only the high-level elements that must be captured within the privacy notice.

As a Privacy practitioner, you must exercise caution and diligence to establish a privacy notice in accordance with your privacy regulations and guidelines.

- **Brief introduction of the organization.**
- **Personal Information We Collect and From Whom We Collect It.** – Enlist the personal data elements collected by your organization and the sources from which such information is collected. The organization may be collecting the personal data directly from the individuals or from some other organizations to carry out the processing.

- **Lawful Purpose for Collecting & Processing Personal Information** – Ensure that the privacy notice explains the legal basis for collecting and processing personal information. This gives the comfort and assurance to the individuals that the organizational business pursuits have a definite legal basis, which can be explained and justified with reason.
- **Personal Data Retention & Data Storage and Security Mechanisms** – The Privacy notice must provide the data retention period for which the organization will store the personal data. This is often a tricky aspect to respond to because the organizations are often collecting multiple personal data elements, and some of the personal data elements may have a particular regulatory requirement to be held for a certain time. In contrast, the other data elements may not have such requirements. It must be ensured that the statement within the privacy notice is transparent, clear, and easy to understand, but also does not create a legal risk since the period which will be mentioned within the privacy notice is an express commitment to the individuals.

  The Privacy Notice must also mention the location and jurisdiction where the personal data will be stored and processed, along with the data security mechanism applied to protect the personal data. It is beneficial to give a reference to the data security regulations that your organization is following to ensure the protection of personal data.
- **With whom does the organization share Personal Information** – The privacy notice must also capture if the personal data will be shared with any entities, their jurisdiction, and the legal basis for sharing or disclosing such information.
- **Will We Inform You of Changes to this Privacy Notice** – This section expresses affirmation to the individuals that any changes to the privacy notice are expected to be made available on the same channel. This is another attempt to empower individuals and ensure transparency around the updating of privacy notices, as it compels organizations to publish the new privacy notices whenever there is a change in personal data processing activities.
- **Your Rights Regarding Processing of Your Personal Data** – This section must list the rights of individuals with respect to their personal data. The enlisted rights must be aligned with the privacy regulations. Organizations must also ensure that there are mechanisms established at the backend to enable individuals to exercise their rights. This book further expands the subject of data subject rights and how they need to be operationalized.

  It will be beneficial if the privacy notice can identify the mechanism through which individuals can exercise each of the identified rights.
- **Touch point to connect with the Data Protection Officer** – Often, privacy regulations require establishing the connection between the DPO and the data subjects. The premise behind such a requirement is that the DPO is an advocate and the ambassador of the

individuals' rights **within** the organization. Quite often, the data subjects find themselves vulnerable to the poor organizational process, which fails to offer a remedy to them, and they find themselves languishing from one customer care touch to another. It is therefore important that access to the DPO is ensured through a privacy notice. This access can be ensured through an email touch point or telephone line whichever is feasible for the organization.

The DPOs must work with other organizational stakeholders to ensure that there are functional mechanisms in place to equip the individuals to exercise the data subject rights. If those mechanisms fail to offer support and remedy to the individuals, then they must be able to connect with the DPO for resolution.

Privacy Notice: Channels to dispense Privacy Notice

Channels and touch points to dispense privacy notices are an essential component to ensure transparency and openness. If the Privacy Notice is not easily accessible by the data subjects, then that's akin to revocation of the data subjects' right to be informed.

The DPO and the privacy functional unit must work with the business units to identify all the potential touchpoints through which the business interacts with the data subjects, ensuring that there is a privacy notice available for individuals to understand the organizational personal data processing activities.

Some of the channels could be the website, mobile application, call center interactive voice response, and customer care offices.

In certain cases, it may be infeasible to display the entire Privacy notice due to constraints associated with space and time, which can be addressed by redirecting the individuals to the website link that contains a detailed privacy notice.

Another approach could be to offer a summarized version of the privacy notice with a link or a note to enable the data subjects to go through the detailed version of the privacy notice. The organizations can also avail the option of leveraging icons and symbols for better and effective communication of privacy notices. However, it is incumbent upon the organizations to then use symbols and icons that the relevant regulatory or supervisory bodies have ratified.

Establishing Data Subject Rights Framework.

The Data subject rights framework is another essential component to ensure effective privacy governance. This governance of data subjects' rights includes establishing a mechanism through which all the data subjects' requests will be handled.

The data subject's rights framework should contain the details mentioned below:

Stakeholder collaboration & Training – The effective and agile dispensation of data subject requests requires a strong collaborative arrangement within the organization. Therefore, the DPO must work with the stakeholders to carve out the roles and responsibilities that each stakeholder needs to play for handling data subject requests.

The data subject rights framework should identify the stakeholders whose support, nature of support, and cooperation are needed for the dispensation of the data subject rights. It is equally important that those individuals be trained to understand the necessary steps to be undertaken as part of the process.

Below is a recommended list of stakeholders that can be beneficial in handling data subject requests.

STAKEHOLDER	Rationale
Information Technology	Providing support and facilitation of any data subject access requests, particularly when they are linked to unstructured data.
	Information technology teams are aware of the path that the data takes to traverse across information systems, databases, and tables.
	Such information is invaluable whenever any workflow for data subject access requests is to be designed and later executed.
Data Management	Data Management teams are often responsible for mapping and inventorying all kinds of data within an organization, including personal data.
	Their inputs can be valuable in designing the workflow and automation of any data subject requests.

Establishment of the channel - The data subject rights framework must entail the channels that will be used by the organization to receive and respond to any data subject requests.

Time Window to Respond – The framework must ensure that there is an established time window to respond to and complete the dispensation of the data subject request. Some privacy regulations stipulate the need for honoring the requests within a specific timeframe.

Therefore, the framework and the procedural workflows should be developed considering the regulatory requirements in mind.

Authenticating the Data Subject – The framework or procedure must highlight the need for authenticating the data subjects before dispensing their rights, especially the rights that require deletion or giving access to individuals. The mechanism through which the authentication will be performed must be captured.

Logging of Data Subject Requests – The framework or procedure must ensure that all data subject requests are logged into a central database. This is beneficial to track the progress of each request, providing necessary evidence for compliance with obligations and to enhance the entire process for data subject requests.

It also provides invaluable information to the management to examine the nature of requests being raised by the individuals and the average time taken to handle a request.

Mind-map to handle each request – Handling a data subject requests, particularly the right to request deletion, access to personal data, and to restrict processing, requires the data privacy function to navigate through a complex terrain of factors before dispensation of that right. These factors require determining if the data subject has validated their identity, the legal basis of collecting and processing such personal data, the location of personal data, and any other considerations expressed within the privacy laws or regulations.

The table below is an illustration of a potential mind map that can be built for each data subject. These mind maps can be beneficial for the data privacy teams to process data subject requests.

RIGHT TO REQUEST ERASURE	
CONSIDERATIONS	**GUIDANCE**
Communication of the timeframe to process a data subject request	The organization must transparently communicate and set expectations of the data subjects about the timeframe for processing a data subject request.
Determine the nature of the relationship between your organization and the data subject.	<ul><li>*Employee.*</li><li>*Vendor staff.*</li><li>*Customer/Consumer.*</li></ul>

Determine if the user has been authenticated.	• Yes • No
Determine the legal basis for processing personal data.	*This can also be validated from the records of the processing activities register developed by the data privacy function.*
Any Additional Considerations for Handling Right to Erasure of Personal Data	

2.3.7 Lawful Purposes for PII Processing Manual

One of the first and foremost requirements within the privacy laws and regulations is to identify the lawful purpose of processing any personal data. The DPOs and their teams are expected to find the most appropriate legal basis/lawful purpose for personal data processing activity.

The failure to select the appropriate legal basis/lawful purpose has a cascading effect on the privacy impact assessments, records of processing activities, and even dispensations of data subject requests.

When a DPO or the data privacy team incorrectly classifies the lawful purpose of processing, they effectively become the enablers to impinge on the rights of individuals. It has a cascade effect, where individuals may be stripped of their right to seek personal data erasure or other data subject rights.

Consider a scenario where legitimate interests' pursuits are determined as legal obligations or vital interests due to an erroneous logic adopted by the DPO and the privacy team.

This has a cascade effect, where individuals may be stripped of their right to seek personal data erasure or to exercise other data subject rights. When this happens, the DPOs effectively provide legal cover to illegitimate or unfair pursuits vis-à-vis personal data processing.

Navigating the terrain of the legal basis within Privacy is one of the most critical and daunting mental exercises that requires:

- A nuanced understanding of privacy laws and regulations.
- Sound understanding of the business objectives.
- How are those objectives being pursued by the organization?

There have been various guidelines issued by the bodies such as the European Data Protection Board, ICO UK, and the Data Protection Commission of Ireland. Still, it is beneficial to transform these guidelines into an internal organizational manual to be used by the data privacy teams for determining the appropriate lawful basis.

The manual must be able to draw the boundaries between each legal basis and provide considerations that must be taken into account prior to the selection of a legal basis. When such a manual is created in alignment with the guidelines provided by the competent authorities and bodies, it helps to synthesize and synchronize the understanding within the data privacy team about the limitations of each legal basis, further helping the DPOs and their privacy teams to select the most appropriate legal basis/lawful purpose of processing personal data.

It needs to be expressed here again that the selection of an incorrect lawful purpose leads to infringement of the individuals' rights and evokes a right to action from the individuals since the legal basis for collecting and processing of personal data is expressed within the privacy notice.

The organizations can benefit from the following in establishing a Manual for Lawful Purpose for PII Processing.

GUIDELINES	LINK
A guide to lawful basis	https://ico.org.uk/for-organisations/uk-gdpr-guidance-and-resources/lawful-basis/a-guide-to-lawful-basis/
Guidance Note: Legal Bases for Processing Personal Data	https://www.dataprotection.ie/sites/default/files/uploads/2020-04/Guidance%20on%20Legal%20Bases.pdf
Guidelines 1/2024 on processing of personal data based on Article 6(1)(f) GDPR	https://www.edpb.europa.eu/system/files/2024-10/edpb_guidelines_202401_legitimateinterest_en.pdf

2.3.8 Establishing Privacy by Design and Default

Introduction & Challenge

Dr. Ann Cavoukian, former information and privacy commissioner of Ontario, had put forward her idea of privacy by design and default in the 1990s, where she expressed that:

"Privacy must be incorporated into networked data systems and technologies, by default. Privacy must become integral to organizational priorities, project objectives, design processes,

and planning operations. Privacy must be embedded into every standard, protocol, and process that touches our lives."

Reference - https://hillnotes.ca/2021/12/09/privacy-by-design-origin-and-purpose/

Privacy by design and default is a critical principle that is pivotal to ensure that individuals' rights with respect to their data are protected. However, the dearth of substantial and objective controls to be implemented makes it difficult for privacy practitioners to translate privacy by design principles into actionable and verifiable controls.

Privacy subject matter experts have long advocated the need to bake privacy into the design as a fundamental ingredient rather than dressing it up on an established product or service. However, organizations are still battling with the challenges to adequately embed privacy into the design aspects of the developed product or service.

Baking Privacy into the design is much more than just integrating privacy into the different phases of systems or software development lifecycle. In fact, it is more about performing a thorough assessment of the possible privacy violations that can take place and how they can harm the individuals regarding their well-being and social liberty.

The real issues creep up with the lack of substantial and objective controls to be implemented within the product or service.

While there has been remarkable work carried out by various experts in laying down the Privacy principles to be incorporated within the design aspects, their abstract nature impairs the organizations' abilities to adequately build privacy into respective products or services.

The abstract nature of the privacy principles allows escape routes for the product or service designers to interpret these principles in their own manner and claim to have adequately baked privacy within their services or products.

Amidst the lack of objective criteria, the organizations struggle to objectively demonstrate their efforts in baking privacy into the service or product design. This often leads to scenarios where organizations may unfairly suffer from the wrath of their auditors or privacy harms may continue to occur.

These challenges have been reasonably addressed through the ISO 27701 Privacy Information Management systems standard, which lays down 9 controls to be incorporated within the product or service to address privacy by design requirements.

In the same breadth, **Jaap-Henk Hoepman** in his paper on Privacy Design strategies laid down 8 data-oriented and process-oriented strategies. These strategies are further expanded upon by 26 tactics, enabling service or product designers to add more nuance to privacy by design.

These strategies and the underlying tactics are extremely beneficial for privacy professionals to implement the idea of data minimization.

Table 7: Privacy by Design Strategies Proposed by Jaap-Henk Hoepman

Data-Oriented Strategies	Process-Oriented Strategies
Separate	Enforce
Minimize	Demonstrate
Hide	Inform
Abstract	Control

Reference - https://www.researchgate.net 1

However, to implement these strategies and the underlying tactics, the organizations may need to rethink and redesign the architecture around conventional databases, network domains, and user domains through which the data traverses across the networks to enable the service.

In a quest to make personal data not linkable with reasonable efforts by the threat actors, it becomes necessary to alter the architecture by moving away from a centralized service architecture to a partially or fully decentralized service architecture. As we decentralize, there becomes an increased need for computational resources, human resources to manage additional service domains, which ultimately adds to the overall product or service cost.

Such challenges impair the smaller organizations' capabilities to commit themselves to privacy by design in their products or services. Additionally, organizations also rely on off-the-shelf software. The underlying architecture in terms of databases and applications is a completely black box to them. T. Therefore, the privacy risks cannot be adequately ascertained or addressed unless the products have been certified against international privacy standards.

There is a dire need to have verifiable and demonstratable privacy controls that are capable of being objectively assessed, validated, and audited to guarantee that the products and services have appropriate safeguards to protect individuals against privacy harm.

Privacy by Design & Default - From Dream to Fruition

This section proposes a process-based approach through which Privacy by design and default controls can be blended into the right stages of the SDLC and project management.

The DPOs must exhibit craftsmanship and expertise to be able to engineer a process where the data privacy requirements are captured and embedded into the products, services, or functions. To be able to engineer a process, DPOs must be able to identify those interfaces, channels, or touch points within an organization where ideas are conceived and conceptualized for further development. It is important to remember that there might still be a residue of channels where you may not be able to add hooks for your privacy requirements. However, it's always beneficial to start with the channels or interfaces from where a major volume of ideas is churned out for development.

The two most stable and consistent channels that a DPO must be targeting to embed privacy hooks are the Software/systems Development Lifecycle and the Project Management function. Before we delve further, it is important to remember that software or systems development is also essentially a project undertaken by an organization. Still, a project may not always entail software development.

Integrating Privacy by Design into Key Lifecycles

PRIVACY BY DESIGN AND DEFAULT

SOFTWARE/SYSTEMS DEVELOPMENT LIFECYCLE

PROJECT MANAGEMENT LIFECYCLE

Figure 12 - Integrating Privacy by Design into Key Lifecycles

It is therefore critical that these two functions within your organization are integrated with your Privacy by Design and Default process to ensure that whenever any idea is conceived or conceptualized, the data privacy function must be invoked for incorporating the data privacy requirements. It is important to emphasize the overall maturity of the Project management and SDLC function within the organization, as the ad hoc practices or lower maturity levels around these functions will exacerbate the organization's ability to embed privacy, resultantly making Privacy by design being a pipe dream.

We must also be able to determine if it's a product, service, or a function in which privacy controls need to be embedded as part of the design.

The conventional SDLC or Project management undergoes the following phases with a variable lexicon adopted within the industry to enunciate these phases.

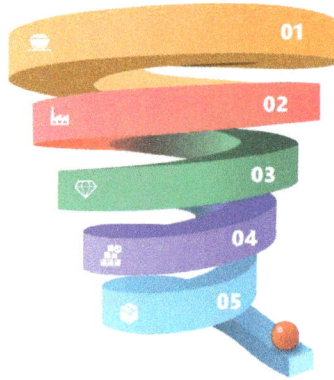

Figure 13 - Conventional Systems' Development Lifecycle

REQUIREMENTS GATHERING PHASE:

The requirements gathering phase is a crucial stage where the Business Owner, responsible for driving the idea forward, collects input to achieve the desired business objectives. Before conducting any privacy impact assessment, privacy professionals must first gain a clear understanding of these business goals as they relate to the product, service, or function in question.

Below are the important details that the privacy professionals must glean from the information being provided by the Business owner.

1. What is the outcome of this product/service/function?

2. Who will be the beneficiaries of this product/service/function? (Individuals or Entities)

3. From where will we be getting the personal data? (Individuals themselves or some other entities)

4. Where will the personal data be processed?

5. Why are we doing this activity? Is it mandated by any law, regulation, or our own commercial or other interests?

The above information can be obtained from the Product/service/function Feature requirements specifications document, which may also contain personas or a high-level block diagram to illustrate the interactions.

The above information will be beneficial for a privacy professional to kick-start their Privacy Impact Assessment and determine the legal basis for personal data processing activity. The privacy professionals may determine the applicability of Privacy by design controls from the below list of non-exhaustive controls. During this phase, you must be able to determine the following (non-exhaustive) details:

1. Legal basis for processing.

2. Does it require a new or modified Privacy Notice?

3. Do we need to obtain consent for such processing?

4. Do we need to perform a Transfer impact assessment?

The solution designers will have to later design their product/service/function keeping in view the applicable controls illustrated below, and specific requirements highlighted in the Requirements gathering phase.

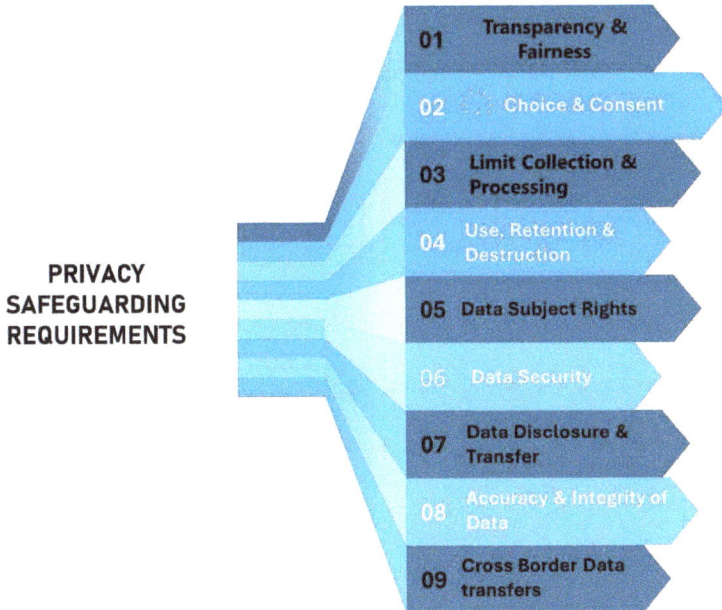

Figure 14 - Privacy Safeguarding Requirements

DESIGN PHASE:

The design phase usually represents a stage where the ideation transcends into a stage to develop an outline for the final product. Additionally, the various production requirements are jotted down along with the identification of the suppliers for key components.

This phase is where you must be able to perform a holistic privacy impact assessment, including examination of the data security controls of the product being developed or deployed within your organization. Additionally, data flow diagrams are critical to pin down the privacy risks.

During this stage, you must be able to assess the consent solicitation panel (if applicable) and how its records will be stored and managed, and how access to data for data subjects will be taken care of.

If the subjected scenario encompasses the data disclosure or transfer to other parties. In that case, the privacy function must determine the mechanisms applied to securely transfer the data to the other entity. It must also be ensured that the systems are designed to maintain Data retention for a specified period, after which it must be securely disposed of.

These aspects must be incorporated within the system logic. To ensure that privacy is baked into the system, the functional requirements should be knitted and tied along with the non-functional requirements.

If the personal data is moving beyond the boundaries of your jurisdiction, then the DPOs and the privacy team may be obligated by regulations to perform a transfer impact assessment as well.

However, if the below list of documentation is not available for Privacy professionals, then it will be a significant challenge to conduct a thorough assessment. It's akin to just examining the crust of the iceberg without getting a fair chance to vet privacy safeguarding controls. Until this phase, it is a safe zone to remediate privacy risks with acceptable costs to the organization, as the actual development of the product has not been initiated.

1. Network Architecture Layouts.

2. Systems and Network Configurations.

3. Data flow diagrams.

4. User Interface Panels.

DEVELOPMENT PHASE:

During the development phase, the project implementation team develops the software or deploys the actual solution that was proposed. Within this stage, the data privacy function does not necessarily need to be involved.

TESTING & VALIDATION PHASE:

During the testing and validation phase, the data privacy function must validate whether their provided requirements have been embedded into the product, service, or function. The Data privacy function may prefer a Penetration testing or Red Teaming report to assess if the security controls are adequate to safeguard the personal data. This stage provides another opportunity for the organization to test and modify the privacy safeguards before putting their product or service into the production environment.

GO-LIVE PHASE:

Once all these aspects have been validated, the decision to move the product or service into the production environment should be taken through a Change Management channel to ensure that all control function aspects have been considered.

Privacy by design is a critical concept to protect the individuals' rights. Therefore it requires imagination and sound analytical skills from privacy professionals to engineer processes where appropriate hooks are placed into the organizational systems so that Privacy is baked at every layer of the product or system's development.

2.3.9 Training & Awareness

We have expressed the idea earlier in the book that Data Privacy is still an evolving and niche field with significantly varying understanding in the minds of the people, which is largely based on their experiences, exposures, and social hierarchies.

When it comes to the sphere of an organization, one of the critical tasks at the hands of the Data Protection officer must be to establish a privacy-centric culture so that personal data protection is etched into the value system of the employees.

Unfortunately, the importance of culture has been reduced to a cliché where its importance is often expressed. But to develop a privacy culture requires consistent, valuable, and intelligent efforts from the DPO and the privacy team within an organization. A thorough and consistent privacy training and awareness program exudes due diligence on the part of the organization is essential to establish a formal training and relevant awareness program.

To develop a privacy culture within an organization, it's important to adopt a two-prong approach within the organization that will enhance the general understanding of employees around personal data protection and will also focus on specialized training, which will be instrumental in raising the competence level of the employees.

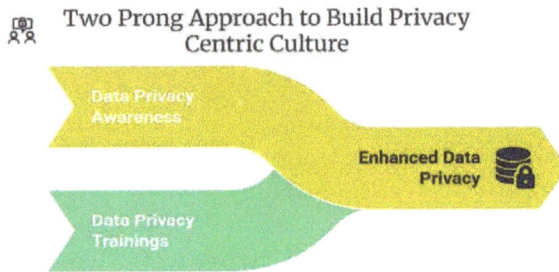

Figure 15 Two Prong Approach to Privacy Centric Culture

Data Privacy Awareness

The DPOs must establish an Awareness program containing various activities and engagements to raise the general understanding of the staff about data privacy. Awareness activities refer to the informal and often voluntary presentation of data privacy material.

One of the challenges that often comes up is the anchored understanding of the employees that data privacy is all about securing personal data. Therefore, employees often have an implicit understanding that the organization is free to collect whatever it wants and store and disclose it in whatever way it deems appropriate as long as it's being done securely.

Below are a few considerations that must be considered while planning for privacy awareness activities.

1. Privacy awareness activities must encompass the explanation of personal data protection principles, their relevance, and significance to their organization. You may benefit immensely by unpacking the various personal data breaches in the past that affected the organizations. Such case studies should delve into explaining the root causes of the data breaches and the financial, reputational impact that the organization had to pay. The DPOs and the privacy teams, however, must exercise caution against indulging in scaremongering because it progressively erodes the trust in the messaging carried out by Data privacy teams.

2. Privacy awareness sessions must not be centered around theoretical discussions with which a common staffer cannot relate. Real skill and intelligence lie in creating an association of privacy with the employees' personal lives so that the employees can identify and relate to

privacy within their daily lives. Employees are more likely to be receptive and responsive to privacy awareness sessions when they are explained how the compromise of their personal data could lead to various privacy harms such as self-censorship, unfair and prejudiced decision making, profiling, etc.

3. The objective of the awareness exercise is to bring behavior modification within the organization; therefore, the privacy workshops and other engagement channels must take into account the requirements of the privacy laws and regulations and explain the rationale and the underlying values that are expected to be protected from privacy laws and regulations. When DPOs appeal to the intellect of the stakeholders and broaden their horizon, the stakeholders within the organization are more likely to respond positively by incorporating privacy requirements into their products, services, or functions.

4. If the privacy workshops are only about storytelling and scaremongering, then the stakeholders will sooner or later feel exhausted and mentally drained. Privacy awareness workshops or other engagement activities must always demand action in clear and simple language. You can do so by enunciating the expectations in simple bullets and phrases and sharing with them privacy policies and guidelines.

5. The DPO and the data privacy team must plan and conduct a yearly privacy day or a week to impart education and awareness within the organizational staff, but also among the consumers of organizational services. It helps to foster a culture of trust and commitment to personal data protection. The Data Privacy Day is annually celebrated on 28th January, so depending on the feasibility, the privacy team must plan various engagement activities, including workshops, games, quizzes, and celebrations for privacy champions' contributions. These activities help to break any mental barriers between the employees and the privacy team.

If such activities are performed annually, then such activities are etched into the minds of the employees, where they expect privacy engagement activities to be in the last week of January. The DPOs may also work with corporate communications to ensure that privacy day or week is featured on the annual calendar of the organization.

It must be noted that eventually the success of Data Privacy Day or week rests upon the substance of the discussions carried out within the workshops or the message relayed to the internal and external stakeholders.

6. The depth and the substance of conversations within the privacy awareness workshops reflect the overall maturity of the function. If a function only continues to delve into the fundamentals of privacy and limits itself to generic privacy understanding, then the

employees will begin to find the workshops redundant and meaningless. The DPOs must work to raise the bar of understanding and depth of conversation in awareness sessions by setting their expectations around data privacy processes like privacy impact assessment, legitimate interests' assessments, records of processing activities, etc., and explaining what is expected from them.

Effective Data Protection Officers (DPOs) use hypothetical scenarios to demonstrate key privacy processes such as privacy impact assessments, legitimate interest assessments, records of processing activities, and responses to data subject requests. These mock exercises help organizational stakeholders better understand the privacy team's thought process, their approach to risk, and what the business must provide to support comprehensive assessments. By illustrating these scenarios, DPOs can clearly communicate the value of involving the privacy function early in the system or software development lifecycle. Doing so ensures that privacy requirements are integrated from the start and do not become last-minute blockers that could hinder the business from meeting its goals or key performance indicators (KPIs).

7. The Privacy teams must be consistent in action and approachable and always willing to take on questions and extend support to the business within the boundaries of the laws and regulations. Privacy awareness engagements are beneficial to break the ice between the stakeholders and to knot an initial connection. However, such connections are only solidified when the privacy team practices what they say and is agile and efficient in facilitating the stakeholders' requests.

8. One of the hallmarks of a smart and effective DPO is to curate periodic privacy awareness to its organizational directors, presidents, or C-level executives. It's important to expand the horizon of C-level executives regarding global privacy regulations and how they affect business pursuits in terms of offering opportunities and posing threats.

The senior management must be briefed about the potential consequences of a personal data breach and the direct and indirect costs associated with the breaches. It's essential to brief them about the aftershocks of the data breach that may continue to surface even in months after the personal data breach has been remediated.

Similarly, the DPOs must highlight the potential consequences of a private right of action or lawsuits filed against the organization.

The awareness around privacy must always be carried out along with the organizational context to ensure that only those risks that may be relevant to the organization are highlighted in front of the senior management otherwise it will lead to mere scaremongering.

Channels to use

The data privacy team may avail various channels to carry out the privacy awareness within the organization and also provide appropriate awareness to external stakeholders like individual customers.

CHANNELS FOR PRIVACY AWARENESS & ENGAGEMENT ACTIVITIES	
Emails.	Crisp privacy messages extracted through privacy policies and guidelines may be transformed into infographics and shared through corporate communication emails.
Electronic Screens.	
Handouts Flyers	Such messages can be relayed through all these channels, ensuring that the message is easier and quick to absorb, demanding action from staff.
Workshops.	Workshops are more elaborate, giving the DPOs and the staff to engage in more substantive and meaningful conversations. Require more time and engagement with stakeholders within the organization.
Quizzes.	Small, crisp quizzes can be used to gauge the understanding of the organizational staff and to incentivize them upon their results.
Learning Management Systems.	Smaller video-based tutorials related to privacy can be created and hosted on organizational learning management systems. You may work with your HR department to ensure that all employees undergo mandatory privacy awareness orientation through these tutorials.
Websites/Social Media Platforms	It can be beneficial to provide awareness to customers and external stakeholders.

PRIVACY AWARENESS CHANNELS

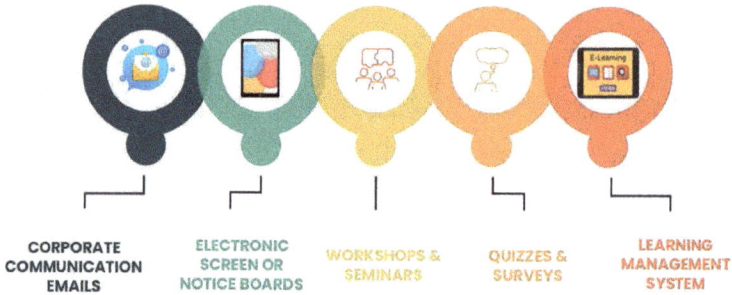

| CORPORATE COMMUNICATION EMAILS | ELECTRONIC SCREEN OR NOTICE BOARDS | WORKSHOPS & SEMINARS | QUIZZES & SURVEYS | LEARNING MANAGEMENT SYSTEM |

Figure 16 - Privacy Awareness Channels

Data Privacy Trainings

Training & education are synonymous with each other. The Trainings are meant to impart knowledge and skillset within the employees that expected to play key roles in the protection of personal data. It involves a formal presentation of material in an academic setting that may lead to professional certification or a degree.

The DPOs must work with the organization's learning and development division to craft the yearly privacy training requirements, ensuring that the organization has competent staff equipped with appropriate knowledge and skills to embed privacy within products, services, processes, and functions.

DPOs must identify the nature of the skillset that they would like to have within the privacy team and understand the functional responsibilities of key players within the organization, their roles, and responsibilities. This understanding helps to chart out the competencies and the relevant training for each category of stakeholders.

Below are the recommended training and the competencies list *(non-exhaustive in nature)* that the DPOs can use to develop their privacy training requirements. Once the privacy training requirements are finalized, they can be provided to the organization's learning and development division to arrange necessary training.

Table 8 - Recommended Training & Competencies for Data Privacy

STAKEHOLDER	DESIRED COMPETENCIES	RELEVANT TRAININGS
Privacy Staff *(Part of data privacy function)*	• Perform PIA, LIA, TIA. • Develop & Maintain Records of Processing Activities. • Execute Privacy Program. • Engage & negotiate DPA. • Understanding of Privacy laws & regulations	• Developing Privacy Program Management. • GDPR, US Privacy Laws. • ISO 27701 PIMS. • Strategic Privacy by Design.
Information Technology Staff • Software Development. • IT Infrastructure & Security Staff. • DB Administrators • Application Support or Backoffice Engineers.	• Embed Privacy controls within SDLC. • Apply Privacy Enhancing Techniques. • Embed privacy controls in daily IT tasks.	• Privacy Technologists Training • Fundamentals of Personal Data Protection.
Legal Team	• Draft & Negotiate Data Processing Agreements. • Embed privacy controls in daily IT tasks.	• GDPR, US Privacy Laws. • Other Privacy Legal trainings.
BI & Data Scientists *(Responsible for performing data analytics and generating business intelligence reports.)*	• Understanding of Personal Data Protection principles.	Fundamentals of Personal Data Protection.
HR & Business Staff	• Understanding of Personal Data Protection principles.	• Fundamentals of Personal Data Protection.

(All staff who are responsible for specific business operations, including sales, marketing, product management, etc.)	• Data Subject Requests Assistance.	• Specialized training on Data Subject Requests Handling.
Customer Support & Call Centre	• Understanding of Personal Data Protection principles. • Data Subject Requests Assistance.	• Fundamentals of Personal Data Protection. • Specialized training on Data Subject Requests Handling.

Reporting of Awareness and Training KPIs.

Once the employees are provided with adequate training and awareness, they must exhibit due care and due diligence based on their roles to protect personal data. The records must be maintained for all individuals who have been provided with training and awareness. The DPOs can benefit by aligning themselves with HR to ensure that all employees are expected to undergo a privacy awareness session during the onboarding stage.

It is equally important that KPIs and metrics are recorded and reported to senior management with regard to privacy training and awareness efforts exerted by the organization. The senior management must be able to facilitate or guide if there are any challenges in attaining the targets established for privacy training and awareness KPIs.

Establishment and execution of a Privacy training and awareness plan is an exhibition of due diligence on the part of the organization. It helps to demonstrate that the organization has left no stone unturned in equipping the staff with adequate knowledge and understanding of personal data protection.

2.3.10 Privacy Performance Measurement

When an organization establishes a dedicated unit for data privacy, allocating financial and human resources and granting it the authority to develop and implement a privacy program, it becomes the organization's responsibility to monitor how effectively the privacy function is working toward its goals. The success of any function is measured through indicators and metrics, which can reveal early signs of issues or demonstrate the function's overall effectiveness and efficiency.

The Data privacy section must establish performance metrics and KPIs that are supposed to reflect the overall health of a system and its capabilities to achieve the desired outcomes. These performance metrics and KPIs are expected to indicate if any underlying function is underperforming, raising cries for help and attention so that adequate support and resources are provided to address the challenges associated with the function.

Before we delve into proposing a list of performance metrics and KPIs, it is important to examine the considerations for developing and operationalizing the Privacy metrics and KPIs.

Important Considerations in Establishing Privacy Metrics & KPIs.

Distinction between Metrics and KPIs.

It's important to have a clear and vivid understanding of the distinction between the performance metrics and the KPIs. Metrics are the vital signs related to a process or a function, while KPIs are indicators that require the computation of multiple metrics to draw a conclusion about the health of a process. The KPIs can be expressed in the form of percentages or ratios, while metrics are often measured in integer values.

Below is an example of a Privacy metric and the KPIs.

Privacy Metrics:

o Number of data subject access requests (DSARs) received.

o Number of DSARs completed within 30 days

Privacy KPIs:

KPI # 1: Percentage of Data Subject Access Requests (DSAR) completed on time within a month.

The above KPI requires two metrics to be computed first:

Metric # 1: Total DSAR completed within timeframe (which could be 30 days, depending on the privacy regulations)

Metric # 2: Total DSARs received within a month

Computation Formula: [(DSARs completed within 30 days ÷ Total DSARs received) × 100%]

The table below draws a comparative view of the distinction between metrics and KPIs.

Table 9 Comparison between Metrics & KPIs

Area	Metrics	Key Performance Indicators (KPIs)
Definition	Data points to measure specific aspects of performance.	Data points derived from metrics to assess the progress or health of a specific privacy process or function.
Computation & Collection	Independently collected directly from processes or systems	Dependent on metrics for computation
Purpose	Provide data points for analysis, but do not necessarily indicate success or failure of a process or a function.	Helps evaluate whether a goal or target is being met or if the function is healthy to ensure attainment of objectives.
Actionability & Utility	Provides insights but may not drive action directly unless they are seen in a context or with other metrics to discern health aspects of the function.	Facilitates decision-making and corrective actions if objectives are not met.

Considering the above context and the significance of the performance metrics, the DPOs and the senior management would love to have performance metrics and KPIs about every functional requirement associated with data privacy; however, the below steps must be taken into account prior to establishing KPIs or performance metrics.

It must be remembered that enlisting KPIs and performance metrics is the easiest task that can be performed. The real task lies in operationalizing the KPIs and performance metrics that are capable of communicating the health of the data privacy functions.

Step 1: Process Identification & Its Maturity:

The first and foremost aspect is to identify the privacy process or the function related to which the metrics or the KPIs are being established. Once the process is identified, then the following must be examined.

- Is the process or the function being carried out within the organization?
- What is the frequency of such a process or the function being carried out?
- What is the maturity of the process or function being carried out?
- Does this process or function contribute to gauging the overall health of privacy?

Step 2: Data Source & Reliability:

In this step, the following must be identified:

- Is there a data source that can be used to compute metrics or KPIs?
- Is the data source considered reliable or consistent?

Step 3: Data's Correlation with Process & Function:

In this step, the following must be identified:

- Does the data have any correlation with the process or function?
- Can we set a target for datasets related to metrics and KPIs?

Step 4: Data Source Selection, Computation Method & Frequency:

Once the above steps have been diligently carried out, it's time to define the computation method for the KPIs or the metric and identify the frequency at which the identified metric or KPIs will be measured.

We must remember that the frequency of all the KPIs or metrics may not be the same, and some performance metrics may need to be measured based on the materialization of the fact.

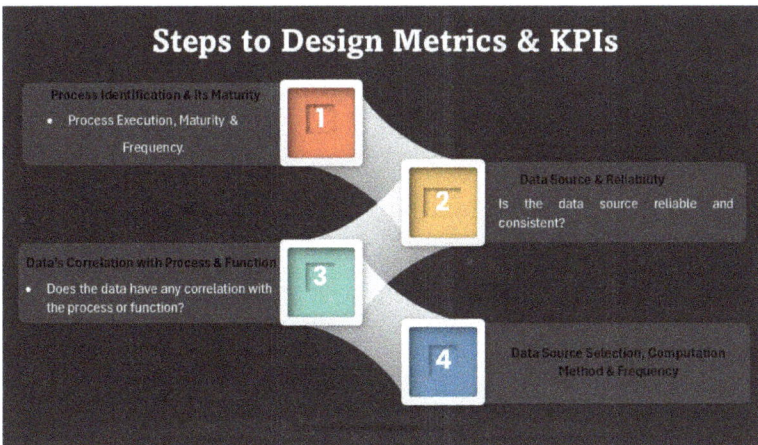

Figure 17 - Steps to Design Metrics & KPIs.

Reports & Audience

The performance metrics and KPIs must be periodically tabulated and reported in the monthly or quarterly reports submitted to the relevant leadership group or the oversight committee established for data privacy.

The table below proposes a non-exhaustive list of privacy metrics and KPIs; the DPOs must exercise due diligence in the adoption of privacy metrics and KPIs, taking into account the above considerations and the organizational context.

PRIVACY AREA	METRICS/ KPI	RATIONALE
Data Subject Requests	Number of DSR received in a month.	Reflects the overall health of the data subject rights function and helps to unearth the causes due to which the function may be unable to achieve its targets.
	%age of DSAR completed on time within a month.	
	Number of DSARs overdue.	
Privacy Awareness & Training	Number of employees provided with training in a year	Reflects the efforts made by the data privacy unit to create a privacy-centric culture.
	Number of privacy awareness workshops conducted in a year.	
	The percentage of employees provided with privacy awareness in a year	
	The percentage of vendors or outsourced staff who provided privacy awareness in a year.	
Privacy Incident & Breaches	Number of Data privacy breaches in a quarter.	Reflects the capability of an organization to identify and respond to breaches in a timely manner.
	%age of privacy breaches reported to data subjects within 72 hours.	

	Average time to report a Breach to the regulator.	
Audits & Compliance	Percentage of audit observations closed.	Reflects if audits identify any functional or procedural gaps or that can impact the compliance status of the organization.
	Percentage of regulatory obligations in non-compliance state.	
Privacy Governance & Risks	Percentage of Privacy risks overdue and untreated.	Reflects the efficacy of a governance and risk process within the organization.
	Number of privacy impact assessments performed in a year.	
	Number of privacy notices developed in a year.	

Measuring Maturity Assessment of Privacy Function.

Another mechanism that can be used to gauge the overall effectiveness of the data privacy function is through periodic maturity assessment against available maturity assessment tools.

The organizations must exercise diligence in the adoption of a particular model with the purpose of ensuring that the maturity assessment model truly examines the depth and consistency of implementation within the organization.

It is ideal to pick or establish a model in-house that is aligned with the Capability Maturity Model Integration (CMMI), which can examine each requirement of a model upon the below identified levels.

- **Initial** – No formal controls exist.
- **Consistent** – The implementation is defined by consistent practice devoid of any approved governance procedures or established process.
- **Defined** & Structured– The implementation is defined by consistent practice governed through approved procedures or established processes.
- **Managed & Measured** – The implementation is gauged by metrics and KPIs where applicable or there exists relevant reporting at periodic intervals.

- **Optimized** – Continuous improvement and optimization of function to ensure efficiency and enhanced effectiveness.

This consideration may appear trivial but carries huge significance because if a maturity assessment tool or a model fails to truly examine the depth and consistency of implementation, then it can give a false sense of assurance to the management about the overall maturity of the data privacy function.

High maturity level scores must not give the notion that the organizations are not susceptible to private rights of actions or personal data breaches. It is the responsibility of the DPO to ensure that such messaging is clearly communicated to the senior management and the oversight committee.

Below are the recommended areas to be incorporated within the Data Privacy Maturity assessment tools in case you wish to build an in-house maturity assessment tool.

- Transparency & Openness.
- Data Subject Rights
- Privacy Assessments.
- Personal Data Breach Readiness.
- Data Security.
- Data Accuracy & Integrity.
- Use, Retention & Disposal
- Cross-Border Data Transfer and Sharing.
- Accountability & Governance.
- Compliance & Monitoring.

Privacy Maturity Assessment Model

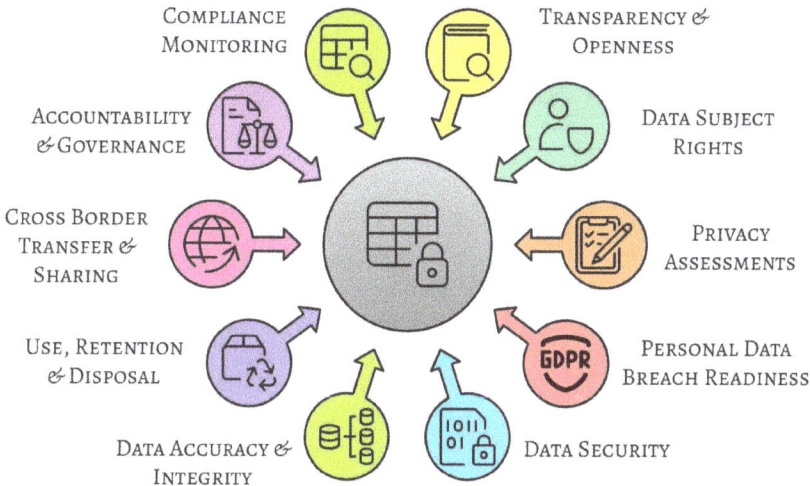

Figure 18 - Privacy Maturity Assessment Model Areas

2.4 Challenges with Human Resource Shortage

Personal Data Protection is still a niche field, and various aspects of this field are in the embryonic stage. Therefore, the industry across various jurisdictions faces the scarcity of qualified privacy professionals. Additionally, the mature and stringent privacy regulations like GDPR and CCPA, along with other emerging global regulations, demand competent resources that can design and navigate the data privacy program successfully.

Privacy, when compared to the disciplines of IT governance and Cybersecurity, is still in its early stages and often lacks standardized education in various jurisdictions, causing a scarcity of human resources.

However, it's important to realize that, contrary to other disciplines, privacy and AI governance are essentially fields that require multi-disciplinary knowledge and skills ranging from legal knowledge, information security, information technology, network and infrastructure security, software development lifecycle, risk management, governance, and compliance. Most of the individuals have often honed their skills in a single discipline, which often debilitates them in developing and executing the data privacy program.

Complex and varied job expectations and placement of privacy at different places within the organizational ladder often exacerbate these challenges. In some jurisdictions, particularly, US, the responsibility of data privacy is discharged by Legal counsel and attorneys while the technical and operational layers of privacy are left to information technology. This inconsistency within the industry has also contributed to the problem of a lack of competent privacy professionals.

Having mentioned the above, the individuals who demonstrate command over these distinct disciplines and cross-functional collaborations with the likes of IT, Legal, HR, marketing, and other departments are often deemed to be the hot cake in the industry, thereby raising the cost of hiring them. Companies are under considerable strain to retain such talented professionals through competitive packages, benefits, allowances, and training.

This variation of skills and knowledge among the existing privacy professionals forces the organization to raise its bar through consistent training and certifications, which adds to the organizational woes.

2.4.1 Mandatory Skills for a Data Protection Officer.

A Data Protection Officer (DPO) plays a pivotal role in ensuring an organization's compliance with personal data protection laws. The ideal candidate must possess a combination of Legal, information technology, cybersecurity, business acumen, risk management, and strategic skills. The DPO is essentially an advocate and an ambassador of individuals' rights, freedoms, and interests ensured by the relevant privacy laws and regulations.

Below is a summarized version of the competencies that the organizations must look for within a candidate for the Data Protection Officer role, whichare critical for existing DPOs and professionals aspiring for a role in the field of personal data protection.

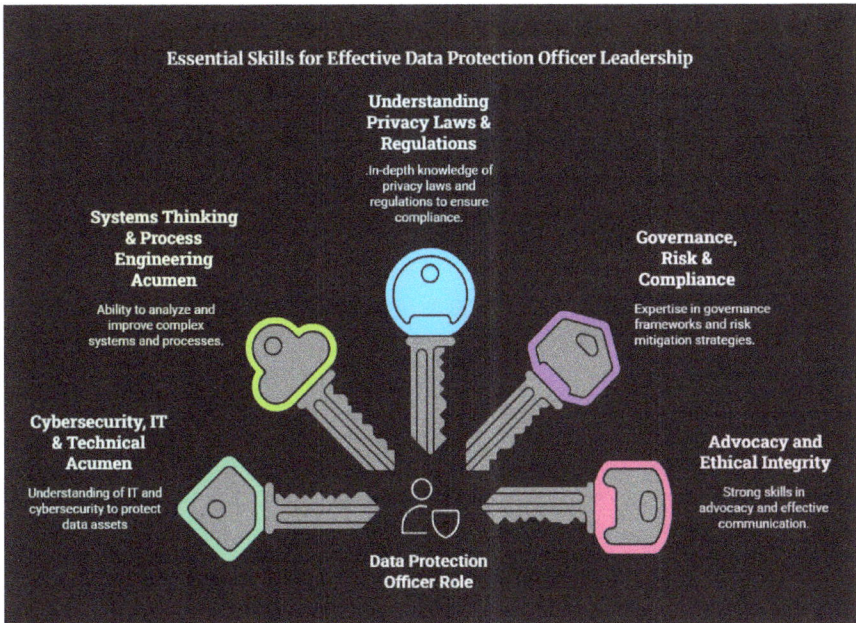

Figure 19 - Data Protection Officer Competencies

1. Strong Understanding of Privacy Laws and Regulations.

A DPO must exhibit a strong command of personal data protection laws and regulations. Knowing what's written in any Law or regulation and quoting their obligatory requirements is one thing, but the implementation of privacy regulatory instruments requires a nuanced understanding of privacy laws and regulations and the holistic eco-systems in which we operate.

Laws and regulations are a tool to manifest the aspirations of society; therefore, the values and aspirations that are hidden within the bounds of the articles need to be understood and implemented through a layer of processes.

Depending on the jurisdiction and the industrial sector in which the organization operates, the DPOs must take into account the privacy laws and regulatory instruments applicable to the organization and ensure that they are able to identify the common requirements between applicable regulatory instruments and the exclusive compliance requirements tied to a specific privacy law and regulation.

121

This competence becomes even more pronounced when the DPO is operating under a centralized or a hybrid governance model, which requires the DPO to have a deeper understanding of privacy laws and regulations incumbent upon their organization.

The DPOs must have a strong command of privacy litigation matters, contract drafting and finalization, particularly during the stages of data processing agreements between the two parties. A competent DPO is always expected to give proper attention to the details of every clause of the agreement and make sure that they are drafted appropriately to protect the rights and interests of the individuals and to ensure that responsibilities and accountabilities between the organizations are clearly defined.

The below non-exhaustive list identifies the major personal data protection laws and regulations found in different jurisdictions.

Table 10 Privacy Regulatory Instruments Worldwide

North America	
United States	○ California Consumer Privacy Act (CCPA) (2018) / California Privacy Rights Act (CPRA) (2023). ○ Health Insurance Portability and Accountability Act (HIPAA) ○ Children's Online Privacy Protection Act (COPPA) (1998) ○ Federal Trade Commission Act (FTC Act) Section 5 (Unfair and Deceptive Practices) ○ State-Specific Privacy Laws
CANADA	○ **Personal Information Protection and Electronic Documents Act (PIPEDA)** (2000) ○ **Provincial Privacy Laws** (e.g., Quebec Law 25, BC PIPA, Alberta PIPA)
EUROPE	
European Union	○ General Data Protection Regulation (GDPR) (2016, effective 2018) ○ Digital Services Act (DSA)

UK	○ **UK GDPR** (Post-Brexit adaptation of GDPR)
SOUTH AMERICA	
BRAZIL	○ Lei Geral de Proteção de Dados (LGPD)
MIDDLE EAST	
UNITED ARAB EMIRATES	○ Dubai International Financial Centre (DIFC) Data Protection Law ○ Abu Dhabi Global Market (ADGM) Data Protection Regulation
SAUDI ARABIA	○ Personal Data Protection Law (PDPL)
QATAR	○ **Personal Data Protection Law**
ASIA-PACIFIC	
CHINA	○ Personal Information Protection Law (PIPL) ○ Data Security Law.
INDIA	○ Digital Personal Data Protection Act (DPDP Act)
SINGAPORE	○ Personal Data Protection Act (PDPA)

2. Systems Thinking & Process Engineering Acumen.

Systems' thinking is one of the most important weapons in the armory of the DPO. Systems thinking is a problem-solving approach that enables individuals to examine and analyze a situation holistically and understand complex systems and the inter-relationships and dependencies within the system rather than just focusing on individual components.

We often hear people exhorting the need to have strategic thinking. However, strategic thinking can never materialize unless an individual possesses systems thinking because it enables the DPO to look at the entire system rather than isolated components and identify how different components of a system are influencing each other and how the impact of a certain component can have a disproportionate impact on the entire system. This can be done by examining cause-and-effect relationships, feedback loops, and evolving conditions that arise from interactions of components within a greater system.

As the DPO must align privacy initiatives with the business goal and the strategic initiatives with the ultimate objective to safeguard the rights, interests, and freedoms of data subjects, it therefore becomes pivotal that the DPO can identify how various business initiatives could adversely affect the data subjects' rights and lead to compliance risks or data breaches.

A DPO that has systems thinking is always in a far better position to predict the occurrence of a problem much before it takes an avalanche effect. This enables them to adequately plan a data privacy program, secure budgets, and stack the various initiatives within a program to ensure that they complement the business strategic initiatives. It also equips them to alert the senior executive management of business pursuits that can be in direct contravention of the privacy laws and regulations.

- **Process Engineering**

Process Engineering is another competence that the DPOs must possess. They must be capable and thoughtful in laying out processes with tentacles to attain the objectives enshrined in the articles of the Law or any regulations. This is the real craftsmanship that the DPO must exhibit through one's imagination, strong analytical skills, ability to conceive and engineer a process within the boundaries of one's mandate, cross-sectional understanding of competing functions within an organization.

The implementation of the regulatory instruments requires nuanced understanding and process engineering skillsets, else they're reduced to a utopian concept, or the organizations end up coughing out money to fulfill their compliance requirements and yet the needle in their strategic roadmap doesn't move ahead.

Take an example of **Purpose Limitation** or **Limit Data Collection** as an abstract concept that is pronounced in most of the privacy laws or regulations. It's always easier but significant to mention Article X states upholding Purpose Limitation, but how a DPO creates procedural layers through which this abstract concept is upheld is the real skill and craftsmanship.

This requires understanding to engineer a mechanism where all initiation channels of personal data collection and processing are identified, and hooks and triggers are placed there through Privacy procedural frameworks to address the potential risk of over-collection and processing.

By doing so, DPO not only ends up translating an abstract concept into a reality or demonstrating compliance but also upholds the values that are hidden within the articles of the laws and regulations.

124

3. Understanding of Information Technology, Cybersecurity & Technical Acumen.

The DPOs must have a sound understanding of information security, information systems, and associated concepts related to IT infrastructure, network security, software development lifecycle, project management, and data governance. While the DPOs are not expected to work at the technical layer but they are expected to work with the stakeholders of these disciplines. Therefore, they must be able to understand the functional concepts related to encryption, anonymization, access management, security monitoring, penetration testing, network performance monitoring, etc.

Having a sound understanding of the software development lifecycle and the project management lifecycle helps the DPOs to place hooks and triggers within their processes to ensure that privacy by design and default requirements are blended within any new initiatives undertaken by the organization.

Similarly when the DPOs are capable of understanding how the data is being hosted on the IT infrastructure and the network pathways that the data takes to move from one system to another either within the organization or beyond, either within the jurisdiction or outside the jurisdiction, this helps the DPOs to correctly assess the privacy risks and ensure that data protection controls (administrative and technical) are there. It further aids the DPO to ensure that adequate clauses or statements are added either into the privacy notices or in the data processing agreement, depending on the situation.

If the DPO fails to understand the mechanism through which the data is being collected, processed, stored, exchanged and disposed of then it makes the DPO vulnerable in correctly identifying the legal basis of personal data collection, framing the Privacy Notices to be dispensed to the data subjects, it also debilitates the DPO in properly negotiating the data processing agreement with the other parties.

4. Understanding of Governance, Risk Management & Compliance.

The Data Protection officers must have an unshakable command of governance as a whole alongside risk management and compliance management. Privacy governance demands establishing a strategy, oversight mechanism, policies, and procedures in place to ensure effective functioning of the data privacy function.

The DPO must be acquainted with the risk management discipline as a whole to ensure that privacy risks are identified, assessed, treated, and reported in line with established risk management frameworks.

The DPOs must understand the compliance obligations and how to transform those obligations into a compliance roadmap to be later executed under a data privacy program.

5. Advocacy, Ethical Integrity & Communication Skills.

As mentioned earlier, the DPO is expected to advocate the rights and interests of the data subjects within the organization, and conventionally, the business pursuits have often put the interests of the data subjects on the back burner. Therefore, it is incumbent upon the DPOs to work towards establishing a privacy-centric culture.

It must be taken into account whenever a new field emerges or a new functional unit is created within the organization; it has to battle for its space and relevance to business sustainability. Privacy is therefore no exception. The organizational units have traditionally operated in a state of inertia, so whenever a new functional unit tries to disrupt or alter that status quo, there will likely be resistance, whether mild or strong.

The character and the conduct of the DPO in particular and the privacy team in general become significant to advance privacy-advocacy within the organization. The DPOs must be able to **consistently exhibit** the following traits in tandem to ensure privacy is incorporated within the organizational culture and becomes part of the new norm rather than always attempting to fight the status quo.

Trait # 1 – Negotiate, Explain Rationale behind your Argument, and Stay Respectful.

No organization is immune to internal rifts. The organizations have various units with competing interests. For example, the marketing and advertising teams would always want to have unfettered access to personal data for achieving their targets set by the management.

In such circumstances, it's lazy to conclude that the other units are not supportive or do not care about privacy. This is where the role of DPO gains more significance as he/she must be able to negotiate and explain the rationale behind articles of the privacy laws and regulations and the potential pitfalls if the organization fails to respect the compliance obligations. Simply stating that privacy laws demand obtaining consent from the individuals will not always help, and there will be people resistant to change. The DPO must appeal to the intellect of the organizational nerve center and explain the possible options and the avenues opened within the law and the underlying reason behind the requirements of the law.

The persuasive reasoning, empathetic listening, stakeholder management, and respectful conduct allow the DPO to wield influence within the organization. When DPOs consistently exhibit the above, the competing organizational units begin to respect the mandate of the privacy function and, more importantly, consider privacy as an important partner in the success of their business pursuits.

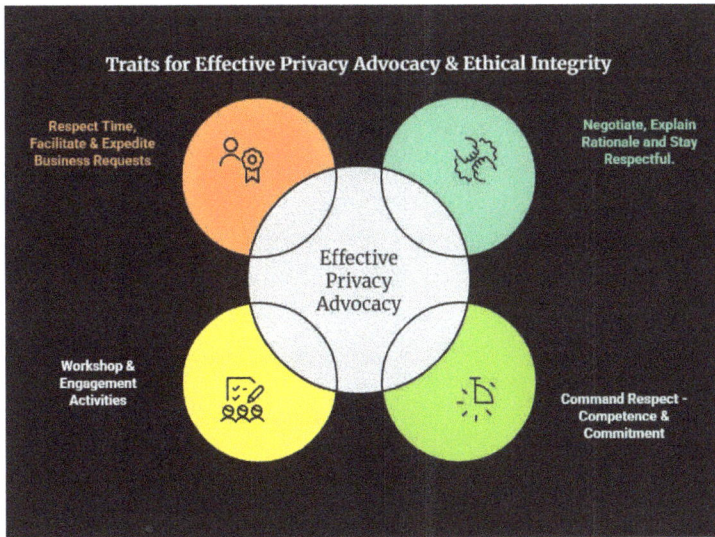

Figure 20 – Traits for Effective Privacy Advocacy

Trait # 2 – Respect Time, Facilitate & Expedite Business Requests.

The DPOs and the privacy team must ensure that they respect the deadlines or timelines of the other organizational business units. Other organizational units may rely on the data privacy function to prepare privacy impact assessment reports and submit to the regulator prior to initiating such processing activities. The Data privacy function must act in an agile manner to ensure that all such requests are handled diligently in a timely manner. Additionally, the DPO must be easily accessible and respond to the organizational employees to support them in any affairs related to data privacy.

While it may seem trivial to the competence of the DPO, it does wonders in establishing a relationship of trust and cooperation with the peers, particularly in the initial months when there is expected to be skepticism and tentativeness around the significance of data privacy.

Trait # 3 – Conduct Workshops & engagement activities.

To establish a privacy-centric culture, the DPO and the privacy team must be able to carry out effective privacy awareness workshops and other engagement activities to ensure that privacy is at the forefront in the minds of the organization and its employees.

It is far more effective and easier to educate the organization about the importance of data privacy during favorable times, as this helps raise awareness, making it easier to integrate data privacy principles and frameworks into business activities.

Trait # 4 – Command Respect through Competence & Commitment

Commanding respect may seem trivial or cliché, but it is the most important asset. DPOs can only command respect and authority through absolute competence and character integrity, which means that they must practice what they preach.

A DPO must act and be seen as an independent voice within the organization for the ethical usage of personal data. This trait becomes even more significant when DPOs have to challenge the fundamental assumptions of the senior management and their business pursuits.

2.5 Guardrails of Trust: Privacy in Integrity Systems

This section is targeted towards processes that ensure integrity and ethical conduct within the organization. These processes may seem trivial, but carry significant tangents with data privacy and can affect the overall organization.

The Organizational Compliance Department is responsible for establishing various processes to ensure ethical conduct and integrity at the workplace. These processes include Conflict of Interest (COI) disclosures, CCTV surveillance, Whistleblowing mechanisms, and Fraud Detection & Prevention.

These processes are essential to establish and uphold ethical conduct, promote transparency, and demonstrate adherence to regulatory compliance. However, each of these processes involves the collection and processing of personal data with significant implications for the rights, freedoms, and interests of the individuals.

This chapter explores how privacy principles must be embedded within these ethics and integrity processes and provides guidance for Data Protection Officers (DPOs) to ensure that the privacy of the individuals is not compromised in pursuit of those ethical ideals.

1. Conflict of Interest (COI) Declarations

A Conflict of Interest Framework is established within organizations to ensure ethical conduct, integrity, trust within the organizational processes, and accountability. Conflicts of interest are more pronounced in government, finance, medical and education sectors as the undeclared or poorly managed conflicts can compromise the reputation and credibility of the organization and further lead to the erosion of trust and transparency within the organization.

Conflict of Interest becomes even more concerning once it's attributed to people in influential positions such as board members and public officials, etc. People in such positions are expected to exhibit high levels of transparency, ethical conduct, and accountability. Therefore, if their interests collide with the organizational interests, then the organizational stakeholders and public trust are most likely to become a casualty.

Conflict of Interest declarations require employees to disclose personal relationships, affiliations, financial interests, stakes, and shares that might impact their impartiality and objectivity. While the data elements collected in this regard may not fall under sensitive personal data, the aggregate nature of various data elements is often likely to raise the risk levels.

Privacy Considerations

It is important for the DPOs to examine these processes carefully because, in pursuit of upholding trust and integrity, the privacy of the individuals making the declarations must not be compromised. Below are the key considerations that DPOs and the privacy professionals must examine as part of their privacy impact assessments.

Key Considerations for DPOs:

1. **Lawful Basis for Processing:** Determining the lawful purpose is the first step with regard to personal data processing. Therefore, the privacy professionals must determine if there is an associated regulatory instrument compelling the conflict-of-interest process to be established within the organization. If there is no legal obligation and the organization has established this process to protect their legitimate interests, then it's necessary to conduct a legitimate interests assessment.

2. **Data Minimization, Purpose Limitation, and Transparency:** If the processing is driven by a legal obligation, then examine if the regulatory instrument has also identified the mandatory and optional data elements to be collected. If the regulatory instrument does not offer specifications around data elements, then the privacy team must ensure that the data elements are linked to serving the objective of the processing and are proportionate.

The personal data collected as part of conflict-of-interest disclosures must not be used for achieving the objectives of any other processing unless legal obligations drive compelling reasons.

To ensure the aspect of transparency, the DPO or privacy team must work with the compliance and ethics officers to develop and dispense a privacy notice that explains the purpose of personal data processing.

It is important to note that a privacy notice is not enough to ensure transparency and fairness instituted within the process. The organization may have served a privacy notice, but the process through which a conflict is identified and qualified may be vague and subjective, which may be enough to strip off the rights, interests, and freedoms of the individuals. It is important to work with the compliance and ethics officers to ensure that there is an effective process to identify and qualify conflicts through an objective mechanism.

The process must also ensure that the identified conflicts are not immediately classified and treated as the violation evoking any punitive action, however the process must ensure that the respondents are given an opportunity to address and eliminate the identified conflict and the organization may only take punitive action through authorized individuals or committees when the individual does not mitigate the conflict.

3. **Data Security & Access Controls:** Determine the information security controls placed at the server or the repository where such records are being stored.

Determine who has access to such records and what privileges are associated.

4. **Retention and Deletion:** Document a clear retention period and ensure that records are securely disposed of after the retention period elapses.

2. CCTV Recording

CCTV systems serve physical security monitoring and to also maintain vigilance over the infrastructure and capture continuous personal data of the individuals in the form of videos or stored images extracted from videos. It is equally important that the physical security monitoring empowered by the CCTV must operate within the boundaries of personal data protection laws to respect individual privacy.

Privacy Considerations

It is important for the DPOs to examine these processes carefully because CCTV recordings may lead to surveillance overreach by capturing identifying features, behaviors, or private activities. Below are the key considerations that DPOs and privacy professionals must examine as part of their privacy impact assessments.

Key Considerations for DPOs:

1. **Lawful Basis for Processing:** Determine if there is an associated regulatory instrument compelling the physical security monitoring to be performed, and if there is, then the

boundaries specified within the regulatory instrument must also be assessed. Some regulations only mandate the monitoring of critical infrastructure and associated areas; therefore, these boundaries must be clearly understood by the privacy team.

If there is no legal obligation and the organization has established this process to protect its legitimate interests, then it's necessary to conduct a legitimate interest assessment.

2. **Data Minimization, Purpose Limitation, and Transparency:** It is important to incorporate such processing activity within the organization's Employee privacy notice, or you can provide just-in-time notices demonstrating that the area is under surveillance. The notices can accompany QR codes with links to the detailed privacy notices.

To ensure that data is not collected from sensitive areas such as restrooms or private rooms, it is important that there must a mechanism be adopted within the organization to approve the installation of the camera. The approval of the installation of CCTV cameras must be granted by an authorized person. The relevant department must also document the rationale behind the installation of cameras and the associated benefits for monitoring that particular area.

3. **Data Security & Access Controls:** Determine the information security controls placed at the server or the repository where such camera recordings are being stored.

Determine who has access to such video recordings and what privileges are associated with the deletion of video recordings and alterations in video recordings.

4. **Retention and Deletion:** Document a clear retention period and ensure that video records are securely disposed of after the retention period elapses. The data retention period must be proportionate to the purpose of processing.

5. **Data Subject Request:** Determine if a structured mechanism exists to respond to access requests involving video data.

3. Whistleblowing Mechanisms

Whistleblowing mechanisms are another instrument to uphold ethical conduct, integrity, and accountability by empowering the organizational insiders to report any corrupt practices. The whistleblowing cases are not about organizational dysfunction or individual disputes or internal grievance, they are about systemic wrongdoing which are carried out under the garb of approved governance to facilitate fraud and corruption.

The objective of the whistleblowing mechanism is to encourage insiders to report such misconduct and to provide them with a safe zone free from retribution where the evidence of the corrupt practices can be examined and acted upon.

Privacy Considerations

Whistleblowing cases offer a significant challenge where the evidence is attributed to the individuals in influential positions and the evidence is data that points towards a person. The evidence may include allegations, personal identifiers, and context involving private communications or other financial information.

In such cases, the DPOs have to protect the privacy of the accused and the whistleblower as well, and ensure that principles of transparency and fairness are upheld.

Below are the key considerations that DPOs and privacy professionals must examine as part of their privacy impact assessments.

Key Aspects for DPOs:

1. **Lawful Basis for Processing:** Determine if there is an associated regulatory instrument compelling the whistleblowing mechanism to be established.

If there is no legal obligation and the organization has established this process to protect its legitimate interests, then it's necessary to conduct a legitimate interest assessment.

2. **Fairness and Transparency:**

Protection of individuals' rights, interests, and freedoms is the foundation of most privacy laws and regulations. Instruments such as privacy notices, data subject access requests, and consent mechanisms serve as tools to uphold these fundamental protections. However, true transparency and fairness extend beyond these tools. They require procedural integrity, meaning that process owners must establish clearly defined, approved mechanisms for handling personal data. These mechanisms must include appropriate checkpoints to ensure that no harm is caused to the rights, freedoms, or interests of individuals throughout the data lifecycle.

The DPOs must be examining personal data processing to ultimately uphold the rights and interests of the individuals, which requires a deeper and more thorough inspection of the processes beyond privacy notice, consent, data security, and DSARs, etc.

When it comes to fairness and transparency within Whistleblowing cases, the DPOs must examine the whistleblowing mechanisms for procedural fairness, ensuring that the identity of the whistleblower and the accused are protected. At the same time, the procedure must also incorporate that the accused must be presumed innocent until proven otherwise. To prove the allegations wrong, the accused must be given a fair opportunity to respond to the allegations.

There must be a privacy notice presented to the whistleblower informing them about the purpose and nature of the processing involved in whistleblowing. The data protection officers must work with ethics and compliance officers to ensure that there is a clear qualification criterion to distinguish between personal grievances, matters of dysfunction or inefficiencies, and reportable misconduct. Such criteria must be communicated to the employees to prevent issues of personal grievances from being reported as whistleblowing.

Another aspect to protect the rights, interests, and freedoms of the individuals is linked to establishing an equilibrium between taking reports seriously and ensuring that the accused is treated fairly and objectively. It is also in the interest of the organization because a mismanaged whistleblowing case can erode trust regardless of the outcome.

3. **Data Security & Access Controls:** Determine the information security controls placed at the server or the repository where such cases are being stored. Establish secure, well-defined pathways such as anonymous hotlines or ombudspersons through which concerns can be raised safely and discreetly.

Determine who has access to such cases and evidence, and what privileges are associated with seeing the cases and altering the evidence.

4. **Retention and Deletion:** Document a clear retention period and ensure that evidence submitted is securely disposed of after the retention period elapses. The data retention period must be proportionate to the purpose of processing.

4. **Fraud Detection and Prevention Management**

Fraud management is another important component of enterprise risk, which is aimed at protecting organizational assets from malicious use. Fraud management encompasses various activities designed to detect, investigate, and prevent fraudulent behavior across the organizational landscape.

Humans are pivotal to architecting fraudulent activities, which can lead to siphoning of resources and cause damage. However, fraudulent activities are only successful due to a series of failures between various controls within an organization, which means that on occasion, individuals' collusion is necessary to successfully carry out a fraudulent activity.

Privacy Considerations
Fraud Detection involves identifying unusual patterns, anomalies, or red flags that may indicate the occurrence of fraudulent activity, which will further kickstart the investigation phase. These data elements also have pointers towards the individuals, which means that the rights, interests, and freedoms of the individuals need to be protected in pursuit of the above investigations.

Below are the key considerations that DPOs and privacy professionals must examine as part of their privacy impact assessments.

Key Aspects for DPOs:

1. **Lawful Basis for Processing:** Determine if there is an associated regulatory instrument compelling the fraud detection and prevention mechanism to be established.

If there is no legal obligation and the organization has established this process to protect its legitimate interests, then it's necessary to conduct a legitimate interest assessment.

2. **Fairness and Transparency:**

The DPOs must examine the processes in the light of the rights, interests, and freedoms of individuals, which are the lynchpin of all the privacy laws and regulations.

The DPOs must assess how the responsible unit will distinguish between a fraudulent activity and any other error or fault in the organizational processes that may lead to a loss. This must be seen from the perspective that if an individual is wrongfully accused of Fraud for operational inefficiencies, then it can significantly fire back on the organization, where the employee may file a lawsuit against the organization for defamation.

The DPOs must examine the fraud investigation mechanisms for procedural fairness, ensuring that the identity of the suspect is protected. At the same time, the procedure must also incorporate that the suspect must be presumed innocent until proven otherwise.

There must be a privacy notice presented to all employees that their information system logs may be processed for fraud detection and investigation purposes. Additionally, there must be a clear qualification criterion to distinguish between matters of operational inefficiencies leading to loss and organized crime. The employees must be made aware of what constitutes fraud to also prevent any blaming and slander cases within the organization.

3. **Data Security & Access Controls:** Determine the information security controls placed at the server or the repository where such fraud incident details are being stored.

Determine who has access to such cases and evidence, and what privileges are associated with seeing the cases and altering the evidence.

4. **Retention and Deletion:** Document a clear retention period and ensure that evidence is securely disposed of after the retention period elapses. The data retention period must be proportionate to the purpose of processing.

Conclusion

The organizational procedures discussed above are meant to uphold the ethical conduct within the organization however, they carry some tangents with the personal data processing that can adversely affect the rights, interests, and freedoms of the individuals.

It requires a sound understanding on the part of DPOs to work with other organizational stakeholders, ensuring that the organizational interests to uphold ethical values are balanced with the rights of the data subjects.

2.6 Preventing Dark Patterns: An ODI Framework for Ethical Digital Design

Introduction

Dark patterns have emerged as a critical concern in digital governance, undermining user autonomy and trust. The term dark patterns, coined in 2010 by UX designer Harry Brignull, refers to deceptive interface designs that trick, coerce or nudge users into actions they might not otherwise take. These manipulative design techniques often benefit organisations at the expense of users' informed choice, for example by inducing unnecessary purchases, obtaining consent for extensive data collection, or making subscription cancellations onerous.

As digital services proliferate globally, from e-commerce websites and mobile apps to AI-driven platforms, regulators have begun to crack down on dark patterns as violations of consumer protection and data protection law. This chapter provides an in-depth analysis of how to prevent dark patterns. The discussion spans conceptual definitions, real-world manifestations (including in AI interfaces), global regulatory responses (EU's GDPR and DSA, US FTC enforcement and California CPRA, Singapore's PDPA, India's DPDP Act, etc.), and practical guidance for detection, auditing, and prevention of dark patterns in organizational practice. The aim is to go beyond generic summaries and provide original, insightful approaches for operationalising ethical and lawful design, thereby enhancing user trust and compliance across jurisdictions.

Defining Dark Patterns: Conceptual and Operational Grounding

From an academic perspective, dark patterns are typically defined as user interface designs that benefit an online service by leading users into decisions they would not otherwise make, often against their own interests. Such interfaces may deceive users or subtly coerce or manipulate them into choices that favour the service provider, for example, opting into surveillance, purchasing unintended add-ons, or remaining subscribed due to a convoluted cancellation process.

In essence, a dark pattern exploits cognitive biases or information asymmetries. Users are pressured, misled or confused by design elements so that their autonomous decision-making is subverted.

Regulatory bodies have increasingly adopted and refined this concept. Notably, the California Privacy Rights Act (CPRA) of 2020 provided one of the first legal definitions: "Dark pattern" means a user interface designed or manipulated with the substantial effect of subverting or impairing user autonomy, decision-making or choice. The CPRA expressly states that any consent obtained through such interfaces "does not constitute consent" under the law.

In practice, this means that if a website uses confusing language or visual tricks to get a user to agree (for instance, a misleading opt-out link or a pre-checked consent box), that agreement is legally invalid. Similarly, California's regulations under the earlier CCPA were amended to prohibit methods that have the purpose or substantial effect of subverting or impairing a consumer's choice to opt out of data sales. This operationalises the concept. It is not just the intent of the designer that matters, but the effect on user autonomy.

The US Federal Trade Commission (FTC) has also embraced this framing. In a 2022 staff report titled "Bringing Dark Patterns to Light", the FTC defines digital dark patterns as "design practices that trick or manipulate users into making choices that they might not otherwise have made". Importantly, the FTC highlights that these choices often cause harm, or at least are not what the user truly wanted.

The FTC and academic experts trace the lineage of dark patterns to decades-old marketing tricks (such as bait-and-switch or fine-print omissions) now supercharged by A/B testing and behavioural data. Modern dark patterns range from outright deception (false claims or hiding information) to more insidious nudges that exploit psychology, for example, using fear of missing out or default options that favour the company.

At their core, all definitions converge on a common principle: a dark pattern is an interface or UX design that materially misleads, coerces, or impairs users' freedom of choice, resulting in outcomes that serve the service provider's interest while violating the user's intent or expectations.

In data protection terms, as the European Data Protection Board (EDPB) notes, dark patterns lead users into making unintended, unwilling and potentially harmful decisions regarding the processing of their personal data, thereby hindering users from effectively protecting their data or exercising their rights. This emphasises that dark patterns often undermine transparency, informed consent, fairness, and other GDPR principles, an issue we will explore further in the regulatory section.

Operationally, identifying a dark pattern requires looking at the design's effect on an average user's decision-making. Key red flags include: does the interface obscure or delay important information? Is one option (e.g. "Accept All") given undue prominence over another ("Reject") in a consent dialogue? Is the user being rushed or emotionally pressured? Are pathways to decline or opt out hidden behind extra clicks (so-called "privacy maze")? Is confusing wording (double negatives, etc.) used to induce mistakes?

Such questions help operationalise the concept into audit criteria. Regulatory definitions like the CPRA's give legal weight to these criteria, and academic taxonomies provide concrete categories (as discussed next) that practitioners can watch for in design reviews. In summary, a dark pattern can be conceptually defined as a deceptive or manipulative UX tactic, and operationally defined by a set of observable design attributes that subvert user intent or understanding.

With this grounding, we turn to how dark patterns manifest across today's digital technologies.

Manifestations Across Web, Mobile, and AI Interfaces

Dark patterns pervade a wide array of digital interfaces, from traditional websites and mobile apps to emerging AI-driven systems. Understanding their manifestations is crucial for detection and prevention. Below, we analyse common patterns in web and mobile UI design, then examine how AI and adaptive systems can introduce new twists to dark patterns.

Web and Mobile UX: Common Dark Pattern Tactics

On the web and in mobile applications, dark patterns often take advantage of visual hierarchy, timing, and language to steer user behaviour. E-commerce and subscription services abound with examples.

A classic dark pattern is fake urgency: for instance, a shopping site displays a countdown timer warning that a deal expires in "5 minutes", coupled with messages like "Only 1 left in stock, order soon!". Unsuspecting users rush to buy, not realising the timer will simply reset (a known case involved the "Hurrify" plugin that reset countdowns to create endless false deadlines).

Similarly, false social proof (e.g. "34 other people are viewing this item right now!" when that is untrue) and illusory high-demand signals are used to manipulate consumers' purchase decisions. These tricks prey on cognitive biases (fear of missing out, herd behaviour) and can lead to harm by inducing purchases the user did not fully want or need.

Another widespread category is obstruction or hindering, where the interface makes certain user actions difficult, especially actions that are against the company's interest. One example is the notorious "subscription trap": signing up for a service is one click, but cancelling requires navigating a labyrinth of menus, dealing with repeated "Are you sure?" prompts, or even having to call customer service.

Companies have intentionally engineered cancellation flows to be tedious (e.g. hiding the cancel button, requiring a physical letter, etc.), leading regulators to label such practices as unfair. In fact, the FTC explicitly warns against "roadblocks to cancellation", insisting that quitting a service should be as easy as signing up.

The Epic Games/Fortnite case in 2022 provides a stark example: the FTC alleged that Fortnite's convoluted menu design caused hundreds of millions of dollars in unwanted charges, as players (including children) found it too easy to accidentally purchase items, but very hard to cancel or get refunds. The interface would even charge users while the game was loading or when a child pressed an adjacent button by mistake, a dark pattern exploiting a confusing UI layout.

Privacy-related dark patterns on web and mobile interfaces have also drawn heavy scrutiny. Consent banners and privacy settings are often designed to nudge users into agreement rather than true choice. Common tactics include: presenting a big, colourful "Accept All" button while burying the "Reject" option behind a grayscale link or multiple clicks; repeatedly prompting users to enable tracking or notifications until they capitulate (a form of nagging); or using confusing toggles and wording (e.g. double negatives like "Don't not share my data") that lead users to accidentally opt in when they meant to opt out.

The FTC report describes interfaces that "highlight a choice that results in more information collection, while greying out the option that enables consumers to limit such practices". For example, a cookie consent dialogue where "Accept All" is bright and centred, but "Decline" is hidden behind a secondary screen.

Another example is incessant permission prompts in mobile apps: a weather app might pester the user for location access continuously with pop-ups ("Allow location access for better service?") until the user, out of frustration, taps "Allow" – essentially a dark pattern by attrition. These practices result in users sharing more personal data than intended, undermining the "freely given" nature of consent required by laws like the GDPR.

Yet another manipulative pattern is interface interference, which covers a variety of tricks to influence choices through visual design. This includes UI inconsistency or "fickle" design, for example changing the placement of controls or using misleading icons. An example is an "X" icon that normally closes a pop-up, but on a particular ad it instead performs another action (perhaps opening a sign-up form).

Likewise, "trick questions" in forms (ambiguous phrasing that causes user confusion) and confirm shaming (guilting the user for choosing an option, such as a decline button labelled "No, I prefer not to save money") are commonly seen in newsletter sign-ups and e-commerce checkouts.

Mobile apps sometimes use forced action, where a user must perform some unwanted task to proceed – for example, an app requiring you to rate it 5 stars to unlock certain features, or forcing disclosure of contacts to use the service.

Studies show just how prevalent these patterns are. In a sweeping analysis, Mathur et al. (2019) found dark patterns on over 1,200 shopping websites, spanning tactics like false countdowns, sneaking extra items into carts, and more. Another study noted that 95 percent of popular Android apps contained at least one dark pattern, often related to advertising and data collection. Clearly, these deceptive designs are not isolated incidents but rather systemic issues in digital product design.

AI-Driven Interfaces: The Next Frontier of Dark Patterns

With the rise of artificial intelligence and machine learning in user interfaces, dark patterns are poised to become even more sophisticated, unless checked. AI-driven systems can dynamically adjust content and interface layouts in response to user data, enabling a form of hyper-personalised manipulation.

For instance, an AI-powered e-commerce site could algorithmically figure out which persuasive tactic works best on each user. Some might respond more to urgency, others to social proof. Through continuous A/B testing and reinforcement learning on user behaviour, an AI system might learn the optimal moment to prompt a user, the perfect wording to elicit a "Yes", or the exact interface tweak that increases conversion, potentially creating adaptive dark patterns tailored to individual weaknesses.

Consider personalized recommender systems on social media or video streaming platforms. These AI systems already decide which content to show to maximise engagement. If misused, they could also learn to deploy manipulative UI elements. For example, a social media feed AI might notice you hesitate when a pop-up asks for your phone number, so it waits and presents the request later at a more emotionally opportune time (say, right after you receive lots of likes on a post, catching you in a positive mood), thereby subtly increasing the likelihood of consent.

This blends behavioural science with algorithmic optimisation, essentially creating AI-powered dark patterns. Another scenario is conversational AI assistants or chatbots that use human-like dialogue to nudge users. A chatbot might downplay the privacy implications of a request ("I only need access to your contacts to help you more, okay?") in a friendly tone that users find hard to refuse. Because users often assign trust to human-like agents, an AI that persuades rather than informs can lead to manipulative outcomes, especially if the system is trained to achieve business KPIs at all costs, such as sign-ups or data sharing.

AI can also exacerbate existing dark patterns by operating at scale and speed. For example, dark advertising patterns, such as disguised ads, can be more effectively targeted through AI profiling. If an AI knows a certain user is less digitally literate, it might serve them a "Download now" fake button ad that the user is more likely to click, whereas a tech-savvy user might see a different approach.

The exploitation of cognitive biases that researchers noted in manual dark patterns could become far more personalised when AI is selecting which bias to exploit for whom. This raises serious ethical issues, as Marie Potel and others have cautioned. AI could create a feedback loop that continually refines manipulative techniques, potentially outpacing human ability to monitor them.

An especially troubling possibility is AI-enabled real-time interface changes. Imagine a future e-commerce site that notices a user hesitating at checkout. The AI could, on the fly, introduce a "special discount if you buy now" timer or a faux testimonial pop-up saying, "John from London just bought this!" to push the user over the edge. Such on-the-spot dark patterns would be hard for conventional audits to catch, since they are dynamic.

It is important to note that not all personalisation is a dark pattern. Indeed, AI can improve UX legitimately. However, the risk is that without ethical guidelines, the same technology can be turned towards undue influence.

The EU's AI Act recognises this risk in a broad sense by classifying AI systems that manipulate human behaviour to cause harm as prohibited practices. While that focuses on significant harms, the everyday subtle manipulations in commercial UX also deserve attention.

In summary, web and mobile interfaces today exhibit a broad arsenal of dark patterns (nagging pop-ups, false urgency, hidden opt-outs, obstructive flows, and so on), and AI-driven interfaces threaten to amplify these through personalisation and continuous optimisation. This underscores the need for robust governance: both stringent regulation (as we discuss next) and proactive organisational measures (addressed in later sections) to prevent the escalation of dark patterns in the age of AI.

Regulatory Responses and Enforcement Around the World

Regulators worldwide have recognised dark patterns as detrimental to consumer rights and data protection and are responding through both new rules and enforcement of existing laws. This section surveys key developments in the EU, US, and APAC regions, focusing on how different legal frameworks define and address dark patterns and what enforcement actions have been taken.

European Union: GDPR, DSA, and Data Protection Authorities

The EU's approach to dark patterns is rooted in fundamental principles of its data protection and consumer protection law. Although the General Data Protection Regulation (GDPR) does not explicitly use the term "dark patterns", its requirements for transparency, informed consent, fairness, data minimisation, and privacy by design provide a strong basis to deem manipulative interfaces unlawful.

In fact, the EDPB's Guidelines 3/2022 on Dark Patterns in Social Media make clear that interfaces misleading users about data processing breach GDPR obligations. For example, if a social media platform uses an overload of prompts or an ambiguous design such that users unwittingly share more data, it likely violates GDPR Article 5(1)(a) (fairness and transparency) or Article 7 (valid consent).

The EDPB categorises common dark patterns in terms of how they conflict with GDPR principles. For example, "Overloading" (bombarding users with excessive choices or requests) contravenes data minimisation and transparency, "Skipping" (designs that cause users to forget privacy aspects) undermines informed consent, and "Stirring" (emotional manipulation) and "Hindering" (obstructing privacy controls) go against fairness and user control. These guidelines provide EU-wide clarity: any UI or UX that nudges users toward more invasive options, or makes privacy-friendly choices difficult, can be viewed as a GDPR violation and subject to enforcement.

We are indeed seeing enforcement follow suit. Several EU Data Protection Authorities have fined companies for practices that amount to dark patterns. A prominent example is the enforcement against big tech for problematic cookie consent banners. In late 2021, the French CNIL fined Google and Facebook €150 million and €60 million respectively for making it much harder to refuse cookies than to accept them, noting that such design imbalance infringed the freedom of consent (a GDPR requirement).

The CNIL specifically criticised design choices like presenting an "Accept All" button but burying "Reject All" behind multiple clicks, a textbook dark pattern of hindering or obstruction. Following this, many companies operating in Europe had to redesign their cookie banners to include an equally easy "Reject All" option.

Similarly, EU consumer protection authorities coordinated a "sweep" of retail websites in 2023 and found that 148 out of 399 sites deployed at least one dark pattern (such as fake countdowns or hidden information), leading to warnings and requirements to correct those practices. This cross-border sweep, under the CPC Network, was partly motivated by new emphasis on dark patterns under EU law.

The Digital Services Act (DSA) of 2022 explicitly bans certain dark patterns for online platforms. Article 25 of the DSA provides that "providers of online platforms shall not design, organise or operate their online interfaces in a way that deceives, manipulates or otherwise materially distorts or impairs the ability of recipients to make free and informed decisions".

In essence, the DSA imposes a duty to avoid deceptive design in anything from signup flows to purchase processes. This prohibition covers manipulative interfaces not already caught by existing laws like the Unfair Commercial Practices Directive (UCPD) or GDPR. For instance, many commercial dark patterns (false advertising claims, bait-and-switch) are already illegal under consumer law, and privacy-related dark patterns fall under GDPR. The DSA fills gaps for platform interface issues that might otherwise slip through.

The DSA's scope is broad, covering marketplaces, social media, app stores, and similar platforms operating in the EU, and violations can lead to hefty fines of up to 6 percent of global turnover. This marks a clear regulatory push to stamp out dark patterns in design. Early 2024 saw the first tests of these provisions when the European Commission sent formal notices to large platforms about interface compliance, indicating seriousness about enforcement.

Beyond the GDPR and DSA, the EU also relies on consumer protection law. The UCPD (Directive 2005/29/EC) prohibits "unfair commercial practices", including misleading actions or omissions. National authorities (like the Irish CCPC referenced in the Irish Examiner piece) invoke these laws to tackle dark patterns that mislead consumers into transactions.

For example, in 2020 the Norwegian Consumer Council's report *Deceived by Design* triggered regulatory pressure on companies like Facebook and Google to change settings that were confusing users into sharing data. Furthermore, design practices that cause "unconscionable conduct" or "false or misleading representations" are pursued under general consumer law in jurisdictions as diverse as the UK, Australia, and even Kenya, showing a global trend that often parallels EU principles.

In summary, the EU has a multi-pronged legal foundation against dark patterns. Data protection regulators treat manipulative consent and privacy interfaces as GDPR violations, and the DSA and consumer laws explicitly outlaw deceptive design practices more broadly. European enforcement, while still ramping up, has begun to make examples of companies employing dark patterns, pushing industries toward cleaner, user-friendly design.

United States: FTC Enforcement, State Laws, and Industry Impact

In the United States, dark patterns are addressed through a combination of FTC actions and state privacy laws. The FTC Act's broad prohibition on "unfair or deceptive acts or practices" (UDAP) is the main federal tool. The FTC has made it abundantly clear that it views many dark patterns as deceptive practices that violate Section 5 of the FTC Act.

In its 2022 staff report on dark patterns, the FTC not only defined the concept but also provided a taxonomy of four categories: designs that induce false beliefs (for example, disguised ads, fake social proof); designs that hide or delay disclosure of material information; designs that lead to unauthorised or unwanted purchases (for example, trick flows, "sneak into basket"); and designs that obscure or subvert privacy choices. Each category was illustrated with real cases, signalling that the Commission has been tracking and acting on these issues.

FTC enforcement in recent years underscores a crackdown on dark patterns. A prime example is the case against Match.com (2019), where the FTC sued the online dating service for tricking users into paid subscriptions via fake love interest notifications. Match was accused of knowingly sending alerts like "Someone liked you!" from accounts that turned out to be scammers or bots, inducing users to subscribe under false pretences. This falls squarely under deceptive design to spur purchases.

Another landmark case is FTC v. ABC mouse (2020), where an online kids' education platform was fined for a cumbersome cancellation process that trapped consumers in subscription renewals (an obstruction pattern). Most notably, in late 2022 the FTC reached a record-breaking settlement with Epic Games (Fortnite) for 245 million dollars in refunds over dark patterns causing unintended in-game purchases. The FTC's complaint detailed how Fortnite's interface was designed such that a single inadvertent click could charge a user, and options to cancel or dispute charges were hidden, calling these practices "illegal dark patterns" that tricked millions of players (including children). Epic was not only fined but also required to revamp its design.

In 2023, the FTC sued Amazon, alleging that its Prime enrolment and cancellation process was deliberately confusing (labelled internally as "Project Iliad") to impede users from quitting. Again, this highlighted that even UX on major platforms is under scrutiny.

At the state level, privacy laws have moved to prohibit dark patterns explicitly in the context of consent. The California Consumer Privacy Act (CCPA), as amended by the CPRA, is leading this charge. As mentioned, the CPRA declares consent obtained via dark patterns invalid. Moreover, regulations in California give examples. For instance, a consent interface that has a misleading toggle or uses double negatives would be considered a dark pattern, as would requiring excessive steps to opt out of sale or sharing of data.

Other states have followed suit. The Colorado Privacy Act (effective 2023) similarly defines "dark patterns" and disallows their use for obtaining user consent (mirroring California's language). The same is true for the Connecticut Data Privacy Act and, to some extent, the Virginia Consumer Data Protection Act. These laws incorporate the concept that an agreement obtained through deceptive UI is not valid consent.

These laws were inspired by the recognition that user rights (such as the right to opt out of data sales or targeted advertising) could be undermined by clever interface tricks, so the laws attempt to stay ahead of that by codifying UX standards.

Enforcement of state laws on this front is just beginning, given that most took effect in 2023. In late 2023, California's new Privacy Protection Agency (CPPA) issued an enforcement advisory prioritizing dark patterns, warning businesses that designs "with the substantial effect of subverting or impairing user choice" will face penalties. The CPPA specifically called out things like forced consent (cookie walls), confusing language, and unequal choice design as areas they will investigate.

We can expect California to bring some of the first state-level cases enforcing these provisions, which will likely set precedents for the rest of the United States.

It is also worth noting industry self-regulation and reputation. Many big tech companies, under pressure from both the FTC and public opinion, have started voluntarily updating their interfaces. For instance, Amazon, even before the FTC's lawsuit concluded, simplified its Prime cancellation flow in mid-2022 after EU regulators intervened. Facebook/Meta revamped its privacy settings to be more straightforward following the Cambridge Analytica scandal.

These changes often occur in response to a mix of legal and market forces. However, smaller companies or less scrupulous actors may not act until compelled by enforcement.

In summary, the United States is addressing dark patterns through a patchwork approach. The FTC's broad authority and high-profile cases are signaling that deceptive UX will be punished, while innovative state laws like the CPRA and Colorado's law are explicitly outlawing manipulative consent interfaces.

The result is increasing legal risk for companies using dark patterns, and a clear direction that user-centric, honest design is becoming the expected norm. That said, it is notable that, unlike the EU, the United States does not yet have a comprehensive single framework solely devoted to dark patterns. Proposed bills like the DETOUR Act, which would have targeted dark patterns on large platforms, have not passed. So, much depends on the effectiveness of FTC enforcement and state privacy regulators in the coming years.

Asia-Pacific: Developments in Singapore, India, and Beyond

In the Asia-Pacific region, awareness of dark patterns is rising, though approaches vary by jurisdiction.

Singapore's Personal Data Protection Act (PDPA), for example, does not name "dark patterns" explicitly, but its emphasis on consent and accountability indirectly guards against such tactics. The PDPA mandates that consent must be obtained voluntarily and with clear notification. The Singapore PDPC (data protection commission) has advised organisations not to use deception or manipulative means to obtain consent, as that would violate the obligation of valid consent (similar to GDPR standards).

In practical terms, if a Singaporean e-commerce site used a pre-ticked box to add users to a mailing list (a sneaky consent mechanism), that would likely be deemed invalid under PDPA guidelines, since consent under PDPA requires a clear affirmative action. Singapore's PDPC has also been proactive in publishing design guidance. For instance, in draft AI governance guidelines, the PDPC underscores transparency and user understanding when deploying AI decision systems – principles that would certainly disapprove of any AI-driven dark patterns.

While we have not yet seen PDPC enforcement cases purely on dark patterns, organisations in Singapore are on notice that any misleading interface that results in improper handling of personal data could attract penalties under PDPA's data protection rules or under consumer protection laws. Singapore's Consumer Fair Trading Act covers unfair practices broadly.

India has taken notable steps recently to address dark patterns both in privacy law and consumer protection law. India's new Digital Personal Data Protection Act, 2023 (DPDPA) enshrines requirements for consent that echo global norms: consent must be "free, specific, informed, unconditional and unambiguous", with a clear affirmative action. This lays a foundation to argue that any consent obtained through deceptive UX (for example, a confusing toggle or a forced action) is not "free and informed" and thus not valid.

Indian lawmakers even acknowledged issues like "consent fatigue" and deception in the digital ecosystem, suggesting that the rules under DPDPA will further clarify what interfaces are unacceptable.

In parallel, India's consumer authorities have been very active. In November 2023, the Central Consumer Protection Authority (CCPA) issued Guidelines for Prevention of Dark Patterns 2023, which is one of the most comprehensive official attempts globally to classify and ban dark patterns.

These guidelines list 13 defined dark patterns in advertising and e-commerce, including:

- **False Urgency (fake countdowns or stock scarcity)**
- **Basket Sneaking (automatically adding items to cart)**
- **Confirm Shaming (guilt-tripping language)**
- **Forced Action (forcing unrelated actions to proceed)**
- **Subscription Trap (making cancellation hard)**
- **Interface Interference (misleading visual design)**
- **Bait and Switch**
- **Drip Pricing (hidden fees revealed late)**
- **Disguised Advertising (ads camouflaged as content)**
- **Nagging (persistent unwanted prompts)**
- **Trick Questions**
- **SaaS Billing (exploiting auto-renewals without proper notice)**
- **Rogue Software (misleading users with fake malware alerts)**

These detailed definitions give companies in India a clear checklist of what not to do, and they tie violations to existing provisions of the Consumer Protection Act, 2019. For example, bait-and-switch and disguised ads are considered misleading advertisements under the law, subject to penalties.

India's holistic approach – addressing dark patterns under both privacy and consumer frameworks – reflects an understanding that the issue spans multiple domains of law.

Elsewhere in APAC, regulatory focus is also sharpening. The Korean Fair Trade Commission (KFTC) in August 2023 released a report on dark patterns, collaborating with the Communications Commission and Personal Information Protection Commission.

Recent Amendments (February 2025): Amendments to the Act on Consumer Protection in Electronic Commerce (E-Commerce Act) and its enforcement regulations, which took effect on 14 February 2025, introduce specific penalties for violations related to six defined types of dark patterns. These penalties include:

- **First offence:** Fine of 1 million KRW (approx. $1,000) and a three-month service suspension
- **Second offence:** Fine of 2 million KRW (approx. $2,000) and a six-month service suspension
- **Third offence and beyond:** Fine of 5 million KRW (approx. $5,000) and a twelve-month service suspension

This indicates a significant deterrent in South Korea, treating dark patterns as a serious market offence.

Australia has utilised its existing laws. The Australian Competition and Consumer Commission (ACCC) views certain dark patterns as violating the Australian Consumer Law's prohibition of misleading or unconscionable conduct. The ACCC's 2019 digital platforms inquiry flagged manipulative interfaces, and in 2022 Australia fined Google A$60 million for misleading data settings, essentially for an interface that confused users about location tracking options.

Japan and Hong Kong have been slightly quieter specifically on the use of "dark patterns" as a term, but their consumer protection agencies enforce against similar deceptive practices. For example, Japan's Act against Unjustifiable Premiums and Misleading Representations could apply to fake urgency or drip pricing claims.

One should also note the role of international organisations. The OECD published a policy paper in 2022 on "Dark Commercial Patterns" advocating for global principles to combat them. There is a growing consensus across borders that dark patterns erode user trust and warrant regulatory action. However, enforcement levels still vary. A 2024 academic review observed "little to no enforcement effort by authorities to counter dark patterns" in many countries and called for more global coordination. This suggests that while laws are emerging, consistent enforcement is the next challenge.

In summary, APAC jurisdictions are increasingly aligning with the global trend: ensure that user consent and consumer choice are genuine, not the product of deception. Singapore's PDPA framework pushes for honest consent and has oversight on AI use, India has taken a strong stance by formally naming and prohibiting dark patterns in commerce (with likely spillover into data protection), and other countries use general laws to pursue egregious cases.

The trajectory is clear: dark patterns are on the regulatory radar worldwide, and businesses operating globally must adapt to the strictest common denominator, which is rapidly rising.

Preventing Dark Patterns through the ODI Framework

Given the multifaceted nature of dark patterns and the evolving legal landscape, organisations need a structured approach to ensure their digital products remain on the right side of both ethics and law. The ODI framework – Open, Data, Insight – which we have developed, offers a holistic model for this purpose:

- **Open** – emphasising transparency, honesty, and openness in user interactions (clear disclosures, user-centric design).

- **Data** – emphasising responsible data practices, minimisation, and appropriate data flows (collect only what is needed, and don't abuse data to manipulate).

- **Insight** – emphasising diligent use of analytics, oversight, and impact assessments to understand and mitigate risks (continuous improvement with ethical insight).

By structuring anti-dark-pattern strategies around these three pillars, privacy professionals and design teams can systematically detect and prevent dark patterns. Below, we detail each component with guidance and best practices.

Open: Transparency and User-Centric Design

"Open" in the ODI framework stands for openness and transparency in interface design and user communication. The goal is to ensure users are fully informed and in control at every step, without hidden agendas or misleading presentation. To implement this:

- **Transparent Disclosures:** All information that is material to a user's decision should be presented in a clear, conspicuous manner. This means important terms aren't buried in fine print or behind obscure icons. Follow the principle of "No Surprises." For example, if clicking a button will trigger a recurring subscription, the UI should openly state "This is a subscription – you will be charged $X monthly" near that button. Hiding such information (e.g., only in Terms & Conditions) is a dark pattern (hidden information), and regulators deem it deceptive. Transparency also extends to privacy notices – use plain language and layer the information so that essential facts (like what data is collected and why) are upfront, with details accessible but not overwhelming. The EDPB guidelines stress detailed transparency regarding data processing and user rights as a counter to dark patterns, echoing GDPR Articles 12–14. Thus, an "open" design aligns with legal duties to be transparent.

- **Honest & Clear Language:** Dark patterns often thrive on confusing or ambiguous wording ("trick questions"). To prevent this, organisations should institute a plain language policy for all user-facing text. Avoid double negatives ("Opt-out of not receiving emails"), avoid emotionally manipulative phrases ("Only a fool would decline!"), and ensure button labels clearly reflect the action ("Delete account" means delete, not hide). User research should verify that an average user understands the choices. A good practice is to apply the test: Would a reasonable user know exactly what they are agreeing to or declining based on this text? If not, revise for clarity. Regulators like the CPPA in California have suggested that overly complex or misleading language in consent flows indicates a dark pattern. Instead, phrasing should be unambiguous and neutral – e.g. use "Yes, sign me up" and "No, thanks" rather than "Yes" and "No (I hate savings)" which injects bias.

- **Balanced Design & Choice Architecture:** An open approach means designing choice interfaces that are balanced and user-centric, not company-biased. Concretely, if users have a right to say no (to cookies, to marketing, etc.), the option to say no should be as easy and frictionless as the option to say yes. This balances the choice architecture. For instance, in a cookie consent banner, present "Accept All" and "Reject All" as equal buttons side by side (perhaps even inverting which side randomly to avoid presumed defaults). Do not hide one in a link or make one button more visually salient than the other. Similarly, for permissions in an app: provide a clear "Don't allow" that is just as prominent as "Allow". Designing with the user's autonomy in mind involves sometimes resisting business temptations to nudge too hard. Privacy opt-outs (like "Do Not Sell My Data" links in California) should be easy to find – some companies put them in a footer or account settings; an open design might use a one-click, always-visible toggle, showing commitment to user choice. Essentially, avoid any element that materially distorts users' ability to make a free, informed choice. If a design decision is being made purely to increase acceptance rates by confusing users, that's a red flag.

- **No Preselection or Forced Choice:** By default, no option that has privacy or monetary impact should be preselected for the user. For example, checkboxes for add-on services or consents should default to unchecked, requiring an explicit user action (this aligns with "affirmative consent" standards in GDPR and other laws). Likewise, users should not be forced to make a choice under duress. If a user closes a dialog or ignores it, the system should not interpret that as consent (and indeed GDPR forbids treating silence or inactivity as consent). An open design gracefully allows a user to proceed without consenting to extra things, whenever feasible, rather than employing take-it-or-leave-it coercion. Of course, some services can legitimately require certain data to function, but even then, explaining why openly can turn a potentially dark pattern into an informed transaction (e.g. "We need your location to provide weather info for your area" along with a "No, use city search instead" alternative).

- **User-Friendly Visuals:** Transparency isn't just textual. Visual transparency involves making sure the interface layout and graphics aren't misleading. Avoid deceptive visuals like ghost buttons (a button that looks inactive but actually is the decline option, or vice versa), or exaggerated visual cues (like an arrow pointing only to the desired option). Instead, use design to educate – e.g. hover tooltips that explain consequences ("Choosing this will subscribe you to monthly updates"). Ensure consistency so users can predict outcomes: for instance, if a red button usually means cancel in your app, don't suddenly use red to mean "delete all data permanently" without warning. Open design principle: The user should never feel tricked by how things looked. If users are often surprised by what happened after clicking something, that interface likely needs redesign under the Open principle.

Implementing "Open" requires cross-functional effort: UX writers, designers, and legal teams should collaborate early in the design process to weed out any design that could be construed as sneaky. Some organisations adopt "UX transparency guidelines" internally, doing reviews for every major flow (especially sign-ups, settings, purchases).

A simple but effective measure is user testing: observe real users trying to perform tasks – if many misunderstand or hesitate at a particular step, it may indicate a confusing or manipulative element. Openness in design not only avoids dark patterns but can be a market differentiator – users increasingly appreciate services that are straightforward about what they're doing.

In line with that, some companies publish "dark pattern audits" or transparency reports detailing how they changed a UI to be more user-friendly (for instance, after GDPR many sites released notes like "we've updated our cookie UI to make rejecting as easy as accepting"). Embracing the Open principle thus builds trust and meets regulatory expectations of fairness and transparency.

Data: Responsible Data Practices and Minimisation

The Data pillar of the ODI framework focuses on how data is collected, used, and managed. Since many dark patterns are fundamentally about grabbing more data or advantage from users than they would freely give, aligning with strong data ethics is a powerful way to prevent dark patterns. Key practices include:

- **Data Minimisation by Design:** Adopt a *"minimise first"* mindset. Only collect personal data that is truly necessary for the user's purpose - and reflect this in the UI. A lot of dark patterns in privacy stem from services trying to collect expansive data (for ad targeting, etc.) by nudging users into consent. By limiting what data you seek in the first place, you remove the incentive to manipulate. For example, if an app can function with approximate location, don't force precise GPS permission; this avoids having to nag the user or hide the "deny" option. Article 5(1)(c) of GDPR codifies data minimisation, and applying it can simplify UX: fewer permissions requests, fewer consent dialogs - and those that remain can be very straightforward, without resorting to tricks. When designers ask, "Do we really need this data?" at each step, it naturally cuts down opportunities for dark patterns.

- **Purpose Limitation and Contextual Consent:** Tie data requests to clear purposes and *only request them at contextually relevant moments*. A manipulative practice is to ask for broad permissions up front (on first launch, requesting access to contacts, camera, location all at once, overwhelming the user). A better, ethical approach is *just-in-time consent*: e.g. only ask for camera access when the user invokes a feature that obviously needs the camera (scanning a QR code, for instance). This way, the request makes sense to the user, and there is no need for coercion - the value is apparent. It also avoids the "skipping" dark pattern where users click through permissions without understanding, just to start using the app. Purpose limitation (only using data for the specific purpose consented) should be communicated - e.g. "We will use your email *only* for sending your boarding passes, nothing else." This assurance builds trust and ensures that later you are not tempted to misuse that email for marketing via some sneaky opt-out mechanism.

- **No Data Hoarding via Dark Patterns:** Dark patterns often lead to extra data collection or retention that the user didn't intend (such as sneaking an email subscription or making account deletion hard so the company retains user data indefinitely). A responsible Data practice is to make opting out and data deletion as simple as data collection. Implement easy, one-click opt-outs for newsletters (no hidden "you must call to unsubscribe"). Provide user-friendly data deletion or deactivation options - and advertise them in privacy settings. This operationalises principles from laws like California's CPRA, which requires providing a clear "Do Not Sell or Share" option and honours user signals like the Global Privacy Control. If an organisation is willing to let users go or say no easily, it has little reason to introduce dark patterns. On the flip side, if internal metrics overly focus on retaining every bit of data, that pressure can seep into design. To counter this, some privacy-conscious organisations set KPIs around user trust or compliance rather than maximised data collection. This aligns incentives with ethical design.

- **Avoid Exploitative Data Use:** Data-driven personalisation should never be used to *discriminate or exploit* in the interface. For instance, do not use personal data to *dynamically alter prices or pressures* in a way that takes advantage of a user's known traits (what some call "personalised dark patterns"). If you know a user often abandons carts, resist the urge to bombard just them with "Sale ends today!" every hour - treat that as potentially exploitative. Instead, use data to help the user: personalising content in a way that adds value, not trickery. It can be useful to have an internal ethics review for any algorithmic UI decision: *Are we using personal data to benefit the user, or just to benefit ourselves at the user's expense?* The latter veers into dark pattern territory. The FTC has signalled concern over designs that *"subvert privacy preferences"* by leveraging user data (like knowing users' tendencies to click certain designs).

- **Data Protection Impact Assessments (DPIAs):** Integrate dark pattern checks into your DPIA process (as required under GDPR for high-risk processing and encouraged as best practice elsewhere). When evaluating a new product feature from a privacy standpoint, consider the interface as part of the risk. For example, a DPIA for a new recommender algorithm should ask: *Does the user interface allow meaningful control over recommendations and data use? Could the interface design cause consent to be not fully free (e.g., a nudge to accept personalised ads)?* If the DPIA identifies that, say, the default option is overly intrusive (max data sharing) and alternatives are hidden, the team can mitigate by redesigning that aspect. By framing dark patterns as a privacy/data protection risk, you ensure they get the necessary attention and remediation.

- **Complying with Global Data Rules:** Responsible data practices to prevent dark patterns also mean keeping abreast of legal requirements on consent UI. For instance, under India's DPDPA, consent must be "unconditional" - so you cannot bundle a bunch of unrelated consents and force an all-or-nothing from the user. If your product is global, you might as well implement that as a standard: unbundle consents, allow granular control. Similarly, China's Personal Information Protection Law (PIPL) requires clear, voluntary consent for use of personal info - and Chinese regulators have penalised apps for continuously prompting for permissions after denial, considering it harassment. Aligning to the strictest common standard (which is arguably GDPR/CPRA-level consent) will automatically curtail many dark patterns. It's far easier to build one high-ethics design than to maintain a manipulative one and risk patches per region or fines.

In essence, the Data principle is about designing your data interaction with users in good faith. If you treat personal data with respect – asking only what you need, giving users real choice and control over it, and not using it against them – you will inherently avoid most dark patterns that regulators and users abhor. A concrete exercise some companies use is the Data Flow Map from the user perspective: map every piece of data you ask from the user, where it goes, and how the user experiences that exchange. If any point on that map shows an imbalance (user not aware, or would likely not agree if they knew), that's where a dark pattern might be present. Fix it by either stopping that data practice or being more transparent or open about it. By aligning data handling with principles of necessity and respect, one finds that dark patterns become unnecessary – users will share data when they see value and trust the service, which is the sustainable path.

Insight: Analytics, Oversight, and Impact Assessment

The Insight pillar focuses on using analytics and oversight mechanisms to continually detect problematic patterns and ensure decision-making is aligned with user welfare and compliance. It recognises that preventing dark patterns is not a one-and-done task; it requires ongoing insight into how users interact with your system and how your design decisions impact them. Key components:

- **Measure What Matters (Ethical Metrics)**: One fundamental cause of dark patterns is organisations fixating on narrow metrics (click-through rates, conversion, time-on-site) without considering the broader impact. As Narayanan et al. (2020) noted, an A/B test might show a tweak (like hiding the "Sponsored" label on an ad) increases clicks, but that metric alone doesn't capture the long-term damage to user trust or retention.

  To adhere to the Insight principle, teams should expand the metrics used in design experiments. For every A/B test or funnel analysis, include at least one metric reflecting user well-being or sustained engagement. For example, alongside conversion rate, measure the opt-out rate or post-interaction churn. If a design yields more purchases but also more refund requests or complaints, that's a signal of a potentially coercive pattern.

  Some firms are introducing "friction metrics" – e.g. track how long it takes users to find the account deletion page, or how many clicks to opt out. If those metrics reveal high friction, it provides quantifiable insight that something is wrong (and perhaps intentionally so). By measuring such indicators, you can catch dark patterns that otherwise would hide behind rosy sales numbers.

- **User Feedback and Complaints Analysis**: Direct user feedback is an invaluable insight. Companies should monitor customer support tickets, social media mentions, and regulatory complaints for keywords like "confusing," "can't cancel," "tricked," etc. Often, dark patterns become evident from user stories – e.g. "I tried 5 times to unsubscribe but kept getting emails." Treat these not as mere support issues but as compliance or UX alerts.

  Establish a channel for the DPO or compliance team to regularly review feedback related to consent, privacy settings, billing surprises, etc. One can use NLP tools to scan feedback for frustration signals. If multiple users describe the interface as "misleading" in some way, that's a fire alarm to investigate that part of the UX.

Privacy officers can also proactively solicit feedback via user surveys or usability studies focusing on consent journeys or account management journeys. The insight gained may highlight, for instance, that users are unclear about how to opt out – an opportunity to improve and avoid regulatory scrutiny.

- **Ethics Review Boards or Committees:** Many organisations (particularly in tech and AI fields) are establishing internal ethics or responsible AI committees. These bodies should incorporate dark pattern review into their scope. For example, an AI ethics board evaluating a new personalised nudging feature should ask: is this crossing the line into manipulation?

Such committees bring multi-disciplinary insight – ethicists, legal, UX experts – to spot issues that a single product team might miss. A board might set guardrails like: "We will not use A/B testing to optimise any design in ways that reduce user control or clarity." Oversight can involve reviewing experimental designs beforehand or auditing outcomes afterward.

Essentially, having an independent check (somewhat analogous to an IRB in research) can catch dark pattern risks early. The presence of a DPO in these discussions is useful to directly map findings to legal risks (e.g. "This default setting might violate the GDPR's requirement for explicit consent – let's change it.")

- **Continuous Auditing and Testing:** It's wise to periodically audit your own interfaces for dark patterns, almost like you would audit for security vulnerabilities. This could be quarterly UX audits or part of annual compliance assessments. There are even emerging tools and research techniques to detect dark patterns automatically (for instance, scanners for websites that identify likely misdirection or inconsistent UX flows).

While such tools are nascent, a manual audit can simulate typical critical user journeys: create account → adjust privacy settings → make a purchase → try to unsubscribe or delete account. Have an internal team or external usability experts go through these journeys and report any friction points or anything that felt deceptive.

Map those findings to known categories (many of which we've listed: nagging, obstruction, etc.) to see if they match a pattern that should be eliminated. Audits can be informed by regulator guidance – e.g. take the 13 dark patterns listed in India's guidelines and check if any element of your site might resemble them. If yes, you have a clear action item to fix it before an enforcement agency or watchdog notices.

Remember, an ounce of prevention (self-detection) is worth a pound of cure (responding to legal investigations later).

- **Data-Driven Oversight with a Human Touch:** Leverage analytics to get insight but interpret it with a human-centric lens. For instance, if data shows 80 percent of users click "Agree" on a certain consent and only 5 percent click "Manage settings", that could either mean the majority truly don't mind – or it could mean your design discouraged the 5 percent who wanted to manage (possibly a dark pattern at play).

To discern this, one could run a trial with a different interface (e.g. surfacing "Manage settings" equally) and see if the ratio changes significantly. If suddenly 30 percent manage settings when it's made easier, that reveals the original design was indeed suppressing a preference – an insight that a dark pattern was in effect.

This type of testing provides evidence to guide ethical design tweaks. It aligns with the idea of "ethical A/B testing": not just testing for maximising profit, but testing for maximising informed choice.

- **Impact Assessments (Privacy, AI, Consumer):** We discussed DPIAs under Data, but here under Insight, the broader concept is to perform impact assessments whenever major design overhauls or new features are introduced, with a specific eye to user autonomy. This could be part of a larger User Rights Impact Assessment.

For AI systems specifically, conduct Algorithmic Impact Assessments that include a section on "Manipulation or Dark Patterns Risk". For example, if deploying a new recommendation AI on a shopping site, assess: will this system possibly learn to recommend in a way that pressures certain purchases (like always suggesting items about to go off sale)? Do we need constraints or periodic reviews of its outputs to ensure it's not essentially creating dark patterns?

Documenting these considerations and decisions not only helps operationally but could serve as evidence of due diligence if a regulator questions the company's practices.

- **Staying Informed and Adaptive:** The landscape of what constitutes a dark pattern can evolve, especially as new technologies emerge. Use industry insight – follow academic research, regulatory announcements, and cases – to update your understanding.

For example, if the FTC or EDPB issues new guidance or fines a company for a pattern not previously highlighted, consider if something similar exists in your ecosystem. Professional communities (like the IAPP for privacy pros, or UX ethics meetups) are great for sharing insights on dark patterns.

In short, never assume you've solved it once and for all; maintain a learning posture. A relevant practice is to hold post-mortems or retrospectives on any incident: if a dark pattern slipped through and caused an issue (user backlash or a legal notice), analyse how it happened and strengthen processes (maybe the design team wasn't aware of a new law, so now you incorporate legal training for designers).

By embracing Insight, organisations effectively create a feedback loop for ethical design. They quantify and qualify how their design choices affect users, and they feed those learnings back into product development. It's about being informed by data and ethics.

Importantly, Insight complements the "Open" and "Data" pillars: transparency (Open) and minimisation (Data) are somewhat static principles to implement, while Insight keeps an eye on the dynamic relationship between users and the system over time, catching any drift towards manipulation.

Together, our ODI framework thus provides a comprehensive defence: Open ensures the right upfront approach, Data ensures the right handling of information, and Insight ensures ongoing vigilance and adjustment.

Detection, Auditing, and Prevention in Practice

Bringing the ODI framework to life requires concrete operational measures. Privacy professionals and governance leads can implement the following practices (synthesising Open, Data, and Insight) to detect and prevent dark patterns:

- **Cross-Functional Dark Pattern Task Force:** Establish a team or working group (including UX designers, product managers, legal or compliance, data analysts, and perhaps an ethicist or UX researcher) specifically tasked with reviewing high-risk interfaces. This group can meet regularly to review upcoming product changes and audit existing flows. By having all relevant perspectives in the room, it's easier to spot issues. A designer might flag, "We have a growth target to increase sign-ups – the planned modal might be a bit pushy," and the DPO can chime in with legal perspective, etc. Such a task force signals internally that the company takes the issue seriously, creating a culture of accountability. It also serves as a knowledge centre for dark pattern typologies and mitigation techniques.

- **Design Guidelines and Pattern Libraries:** Create internal design guidelines that explicitly call out dark patterns to avoid and, conversely, recommend "bright patterns" (ethical design patterns). For example, have a guideline like "Opt-out processes must not exceed two clicks" or "No use of negative emotional language to coerce consent." Provide illustrated dos and don'ts, e.g. show an example of a bad cookie banner and then the corrected version. Embed these in the UX team's resources and training. Many organisations already have accessibility and usability guidelines; adding an anti-dark-pattern section is a logical extension. A pattern library can include pre-approved components for things like consent modals, so teams don't create their own possibly problematic version from scratch. Standardising on user-friendly components reduces the chance of rogue dark patterns emerging in one corner of the product. This also aligns with Privacy by Design principles, which encourage baking compliance and ethics into design standards.

- **Training and Awareness:** Conduct training sessions for product and design teams on dark patterns – what they are, why they harm users and violate laws, and how to avoid them. Use real examples (anonymised or from competitors) to illustrate. Training can also highlight cognitive biases (like status quo bias, scarcity effect) so designers understand the psychological levers and use them responsibly. Encourage teams to think, "Would I feel comfortable explaining this design to a regulator or the press?" If not, it likely needs change. For AI developers, include modules on how algorithms might inadvertently learn to manipulate (e.g. maximising engagement by exploiting vulnerabilities). Equipping teams with this knowledge makes them the first line of defence. In many cases, designers don't intend to make dark patterns – they fall into it due to lack of awareness or pressure. Training can inoculate against that.

- **User Testing with a Diverse Audience:** When launching or modifying key flows, perform user testing specifically to catch dark pattern effects. Recruit users of varying tech-savviness, ages, etc., because something obvious to a power user might trick a novice. Have them perform tasks (subscribe, opt out, buy and cancel, set privacy preferences) and observe if they struggle or misunderstand. Afterward, interview them: Did you feel in control? Was anything confusing or pushing you? Their feedback can validate that your "Open" transparency efforts are working – or reveal where things are still too convoluted. Pay attention especially if users express surprise ("Oh, I didn't realise I agreed to that!") – that pinpoints a transparency failure. Ensure testers include potentially vulnerable users (e.g. older adults, kids or teens if your service is for them), as dark patterns often prey on those less able to parse tricky UIs (the FTC report noted designs pressuring children via cartoon characters – confirm that your designs don't inadvertently do similar). Incorporating usability testing findings will refine the product and provide evidence of good faith if ever questioned legally.

- **Monitor and Share Regulatory Developments:** Dedicate someone (or a team) to track new laws, guidelines, and enforcement actions globally regarding interface design. For example, when the EDPB issued the social media dark patterns guidelines in 2022, a DPO could summarise the key points for design teams, e.g. avoid "deceptive snugness" (where a default choice is overly cosy to user preferences but is the more intrusive one) – our account sign-up might be doing that by pre-ticking the newsletter box; let's change that. Similarly, as California's CPPA releases guidance or as the Indian CCPA enforces its dark pattern rules, incorporate those lessons. Having a quarterly briefing or newsletter internally can keep teams up to date. Furthermore, share these insights beyond the privacy team – with marketing, with growth teams – so everyone knows the rules of the road. A culture that treats user trust and compliance as everyone's responsibility will collectively guard against dark patterns.

- **Scenario Planning and Red Teaming:** Try a "think like the enemy" exercise: if you were a growth hacker with no scruples, how might you design a flow to force user behaviour? List those sneaky ideas – then ensure your designs do the opposite. This can be a fun but enlightening workshop. Alternatively, use red-teaming: assign someone to intentionally find loopholes in your interface where one could introduce a dark pattern that bypasses current checks. Their job is to attempt to design a deceptive version and see if the process catches it – if it doesn't, that indicates a gap in oversight. This approach, borrowed from security, can highlight weak points in your design governance.

- **Public Commitments and Transparency Reports:** As an advanced measure, companies can make public commitments to ethical design (similar to pledges on AI ethics). For instance, publish a brief statement: "We commit not to use dark patterns. We will never make it harder to cancel than to sign up," etc. Publicising such a stance adds accountability – both externally and internally – because failing to uphold it can lead to public criticism. Some organisations might even submit to third-party audits or certifications for user-centric design. Additionally, publishing transparency reports about user choices can be insightful. For example, report what percentage of users opt out of certain data uses. If those numbers are high, it assures the public that users truly have a choice (and conversely, if near zero, one should introspect if the choice was real or buried).

- **Iterate and Improve:** Prevention is an ongoing process. Use all the data from the above methods to continuously improve. If an audit finds a problem, don't just fix that instance – ask how it happened and strengthen guidelines or training. If a regulator points out an issue (even informally), use that insight across all products. Over time, patterns will emerge, and you can address root causes. For instance, you might realise a particular business KPI consistently leads teams to propose dark patterns (say, an OKR to increase email captures by X percent tempted a team to use a sneaky default opt-in). The solution might be to adjust the KPI to focus on quality of sign-ups over quantity. By aligning business objectives with user trust (perhaps measure active subscribers rather than total emails collected), you remove the conflict that breeds dark patterns.

Ultimately, preventing dark patterns is about operationalising empathy and ethics in design and data practices. It's ensuring that the organisation's practices live up to its values and legal obligations at every level, from strategic goals down to UI text.

Our ODI framework provides guiding principles, and the strategies above translate them into day-to-day practice. By viewing users as partners to empower – rather than subjects to be manipulated – companies not only avoid legal pitfalls but also build long-term loyalty and brand reputation. As regulatory pressures mount and user awareness grows, those organisations that have genuinely ingrained dark pattern prevention will stand out and thrive in the new era of trustworthy digital services.

Conclusion

Dark patterns represent the antithesis of user-centric, fair design. They exploit psychological and informational asymmetries to benefit organisations at the cost of user autonomy and privacy. However, as we have explored, a combination of evolving global regulations and proactive ethical governance is making these tactics increasingly untenable. Privacy and AI professionals are at the forefront of this shift, tasked with transforming abstract principles of transparency, fairness, and accountability into concrete design and policy outcomes.

By using the ODI framework – Open interfaces that prioritise transparency and user understanding, Data practices that respect consent and minimise exploitation, and Insight mechanisms that continually assess and correct course – organisations can operationalise the prevention of dark patterns. This approach requires not just one-time fixes, but a cultural and procedural commitment to ethical design. From brainstorming to deployment and beyond, the user's genuine interest must be a lodestar. The best practices and use cases discussed, spanning web design, mobile apps, and AI systems, illustrate that it is indeed possible to offer user choice and still achieve business goals. In fact, doing so fosters trust, which is increasingly a competitive advantage.

Regulators worldwide – from the EU's GDPR and DSA and detailed EDPB guidelines, to the FTC's aggressive enforcement, to pioneering laws in California, Singapore, India, and others – are converging on the idea that manipulative design has no place in lawful, modern digital services. They are providing both the stick (fines, penalties) and the carrot (clear guidelines for compliant design). Privacy officers and compliance leads should leverage this external pressure as internal leverage to champion better practices. Where enforcement is still nascent, organisations should not wait. The writing is on the wall that dark patterns will eventually be exposed and penalised, as seen in cases like Epic Games and Match.com in the US and cookie consent violations in the EU.

Perhaps most importantly, moving away from dark patterns aligns with the principle of respect for user autonomy and dignity, which underpins not only laws but also the societal licence to operate in the digital economy. In an age of AI, where systems can easily tilt into opaque persuasion, doubling down on transparency and user agency is crucial to avoid a techlash or loss of user trust. Privacy and AI governance professionals can bring new thinking and value by crafting organisation-specific frameworks that incorporate legal requirements, ethical design, and innovative oversight (such as the ODI model extended in this chapter). Through rigorous audits, thoughtful design, and ongoing monitoring, they can ensure their organisations are not just avoiding legal risk but actually leading in ethical tech governance.

In conclusion, preventing dark patterns is both an art and a science – an art of empathetic design and a science of analytics and legal compliance. It requires vigilance and creativity, but the reward is a digital environment where users genuinely trust that they will not be misled or coerced – where "agree" truly means agree, and "no" truly means no, without subtext or trickery. Achieving this will differentiate the winners in an era of increasing digital scrutiny. By championing openness, responsible data use, and insightful oversight, we ensure that user autonomy is preserved as a core value of digital innovation, and we fulfil our roles as stewards of ethical and lawful technology.

The challenge of dark patterns can be overcome by shining a light – through transparency, integrity, and insight – so that the digital interfaces of tomorrow are open, fair, and worthy of users' trust.

SECTION III
DATA PRIVACY
OPERATIONS

3.1 Establishing Records of Processing Activities (RoPA)

The records of processing activities are required to be established as a regulatory requirement in some of the privacy regulatory instruments.

EU – GDPR particularly mandates establishing a records of processing activities. The RoPA is essentially an inventory of all personal data processing activities undertaken by an organization. While all the privacy regulatory instruments may not explicitly require establishing and maintaining records of personal data processing activities, it serves a critical role in ensuring that organizational pursuits that involve personal data processing are documented. Each processing activity has a definite lawful purpose.

The records of processing activities help the organizations exhibit clear mapping and visibility of how personal data flows through various information systems, either within the organization or outside, either within the jurisdiction or beyond, along with the legal basis for such processing.

In some jurisdictions, the supervisory authorities may request disclosures around personal data processing activities through the RoPA. Therefore such records offer tangible evidence of an organization's commitment to privacy principles and regulatory compliance.

Below are the two trigger points that often require the creation of records of personal data processing activities within an organization.

Trigger # 1 – When there aren't any records of personal data processing activities maintained within the organization, the data privacy team will be expected to build such register that keeps all such information. This is often experienced when data privacy is a newly established division or a unit within the organization.

Trigger # 2 – When there are records of personal data processing activities maintained, however, the nature of personal data processing is changed, or a new personal data processing activity has been initiated. In such cases, the data privacy unit will be required to update the records of processing activities.

The Data Privacy teams must adopt a collaborative approach by inviting business stakeholders and information technology counterparts to understand the purpose of personal data processing and how such processing is taking place. The information technology staff can provide a deeper understanding of the aspect of personal data processing , which can be beneficial for privacy teams to understand if any personal data processing is being transferred to any external parties or being processed outside the jurisdiction, particularly when the personal data processing is carried out on cloud infrastructure.

Once the records of personal data processing activities are established then they must be sent to the business owners that are responsible for personal data processing activities to review, validate, and confirm the records of personal data processing activities undertaken by their department. This ensures transparency and accountability between the stakeholders.

It is also beneficial to perform a periodic review of the established personal data processing activities records along with the business counterparts to ensure that such records are current and updated. This practice ensures that any personal data processing activities that are either abandoned or added are duly reflected in the RoPA.

Organizations often resort to privacy management software to refine and enhance the creation and maintenance of personal data processing records. Such technological solutions can automate specific aspects of recording personal data processing activities and further aid in creating data flow diagrams that can be beneficial to explain how the personal data is traversing across the information systems and boundaries within or outside the organization.

It must be taken into consideration that technological solutions can only support in enhancing and refining the process of establishing and maintaining RoPA, but if the record keeping activity is done erroneously, the utility of technological solutions is diminished. The organizations must combine technological solutions with competent and knowledgeable privacy professionals who can understand various facets of personal data processing activities and adequately record them in the register.

Below are the core elements that we recommend be maintained for effective records of personal data processing activities within your organization.

Table 11 - Essential Elements to record in the personal data processing activities register.

ESSENTIAL ELEMENTS IN RECORDS OF PROCESSING ACTIVITIES	
ELEMENTS	**RATIONALE**
Department/Unit/Section	Helps to identify the business owner or the beneficiary of the processing within the organization.
Nature & Purpose of Processing	To identify the nature of processing and the expected objectives of such PII processing.
Types of Personal data processed.	Enlisting all the PII categories being processed as part of this activity helps to

	understand if there is any sensitive PII involved in processing, and subsequently it helps to qualify an appropriate legal basis for PII processing. Example: National ID, Date of Birth, Nationality, Gender, Biometric information, Preferences, etc.
Group of people to whom the personal data relates.	To identify whether the data subjects are internal employees, contractors or vendors, customers, beneficiaries of the services, etc.
Recipients of Personal data	By identifying the recipients of the personal data, it helps to assess the risk factor if the personal data is traversing the bounds of the organization or beyond, and also if it is traversing beyond jurisdictions.
Lawful Purpose of PII Processing	This is a critical element in RoPA that qualifies the lawful purpose of processing. DPOs must exercise caution in selecting the most appropriate legal basis in accordance with the regulatory boundaries. The DPOs must demonstrate due care and due diligence in selecting the appropriate legal basis, as the dispensation of the data subject requests can be affected due to inappropriate determination of the lawful purpose. Documenting the lawful purpose within the RoPA also helps to hold the organizations

	accountable, especially when the RoPAs are requested by the regulatory authorities for examination. The DPOs and the organizations can then be questioned for the selection of a specific lawful purpose identified with respect to personal data processing.
Role of the organization in PII processing.	To identify if the organization is acting as a controller or processor in the personal data processing activity.
Data Owners	This helps to identify the business owner within the organization. The objective over here is to enlist the role or the name of the person who is the head or chief of the relevant department benefiting from personal data processing.
Data Retention Period	Data retention periods are essentially a commitment to the individuals about the storage of their personal data.

Maintaining records of data retention periods within the processing activities register helps to hold the organization accountable to adhere to the data retention periods marked out. When any privacy audits are being performed, the auditors may request RoPA and demand to exhibit adherence to the data retention periods identified within RoPA.

It is incumbent upon DPOs to ensure that these data retention periods are accurate, reviewed, and endorsed by the data owners. The DPOs must also work with other organizational stakeholders to explain to |

	them the need to dispose of the data once the data retention period expires.
	There must be an established and defined mechanism within the organization to ensure that personal data is systemically disposed of at the conclusion of the data retention periods.
Is the personal data shared outside the organization	This information allows the organization to determine which processing activities involve sharing or transferring personal data beyond its boundaries. Documenting such information is essential to facilitate the Privacy impact assessment and to qualify any risks that may occur.
Identify the external party with whom personal data is shared	Enlisting the name of the entity helps provide more clarity to the previous element.
Is Personal data shared outside the jurisdiction	This information helps the organization to identify which processing activities involve the sharing or transferring of personal data beyond the jurisdiction. Documenting such information is essential to facilitate the Transfer impact assessment and to qualify any risks that may occur.
Identify the external party beyond jurisdiction with whom personal data is shared.	Enlisting the name of the entity helps provide more clarity to the previous element.

Identify the lawful purpose of sharing PII beyond jurisdiction	Certain regulatory instruments require documenting the lawful purpose of processing even when data is sent beyond jurisdiction. This can be helpful in drafting effective Data processing agreements and ensuring that the data subject rights are well-protected and enforced.
Technical and organizational measures.	Brief information about the administrative and technical controls implemented by the organization to protect the personal data being processed.

We recommend that the summarized results of the records of processing activities are communicated to the management oversight committee to help them understand the landscape of personal data processing, the various legal basis for personal data processing and their implications, the number of personal data processing activities where the personal data is traversing across different jurisdictions and the possible impact of such transfer on the business.

3.2 Personal Data Transfers Beyond Jurisdictions

Personal data transfers have been a bone of contention for businesses, particularly for privacy personnel. In today's world, virtually no trade can be possible without the exchange and transfer of personal data beyond jurisdiction.

Before we delve into the solutions, it's important for the privacy professionals to understand the genesis of data sovereignty and the implications for poorer countries.

Data Sovereignty has emerged as a critical element with the increased digitalization pursuits by countries as governments and private organizations began to digitize government records and transactions, including financial, medical, and communications records, along with the physical locations of individuals. This ability to record and process data elements added to the nation's ability to create value within society. However, in the initial days of the internet, when the data was not ubiquitously available and largely stored on centralized data centers within the national borders of the countries, the risk of personal data transfer was almost non-existent.

With the better trade integration between the nations and the rise of increased global connectivity powered through advanced network throughputs and through cloud computing capabilities, data availability became borderless. This dimension also allowed the nations to look at the data from a strategic national interest.

The citizens and the residents of the country expect their governments to handle their data will be handled in a fair, legal, and secure manner. Therefore, the governments are rightfully concerned when it comes to jurisdictional aspects over personal data transfers. If personal data were stored abroad, it may fall under certain legal or governmental agencies, exposing sensitive personal information to other nations' surveillance or legal processes.

This rightful concern is further intensified if the personal data is being stored in an adversarial country or a region where there are no privacy laws or regulations, or their implementation is inconsistent or ineffective. Additionally, the weak government structures, poor implementation of rules of law, independence of the judiciary, and its failure to get its verdicts implemented contribute to the concerns associated with the transfer and storing personal data in foreign jurisdictions.

The absence of adequate measures or options within the range of the government is likely to make them feeble in protecting the rights, interests, and freedoms of their citizens.

Approach to Deal with Personal Data Transfer Beyond Jurisdiction

Various jurisdictions have their own regulatory requirements to gauge the risks associated with the transfer of personal data. Therefore this chapter will not profess any exhaustive approach to privacy professionals to assess the risks and take measures accordingly.

It's imperative to first determine the jurisdiction in which your organization operates and the applicable regulations on your organization. It is equally important to identify the flow of personal data across the jurisdictions and the transits that the personal data may take before landing at its eventual destination.

As a Data Privacy professional, you must identify the options provided by the regulations to exercise personal data transfers and to guard against the blanket or conditional prohibitions expressed within the regulations.

Below are the high-level guidelines that you can follow to assess any personal data transfer activities beyond your jurisdiction. The below steps offer a consolidated view of **practical steps** required or recommended by regulations such as the EU GDPR, UK GDPR, Singapore PDPA, Brazil's LGPD, Canada's PIPEDA, California's CCPA/CPRA, and others:

Option 1: Determine if the Destination country is within the Adequacy list

If your regulatory authorities have issued a list of countries that are deemed to have adequacy, then you can proceed without additional appropriate safeguards. The EU and UK maintain a list of "adequate" countries with appropriate personal data protection offered by the host countries. The EU Commission issues the list. It is also important to state that since the EU GDPR is attributed as the gold standard for personal data protection across the globe, the other privacy laws and regulations also resonate with the same theme through their provisions and clauses.

As Privacy professionals, it is important to keep an eye on the adequacy decisions passed by the relevant authorities to ensure that personal data is not transferred to riskier jurisdictions.

The adequacy decisions issued by the EU Commission are centered around the following considerations.

1. Rule of Law, Legal Framework & Judicial Independence – Determining the situation regarding the rule of law within the country, the existing legal frameworks, particularly data privacy laws or regulations. The presence of an independent judiciary ensures that there exists a fair and transparent mechanism to seek redress for the damage caused to individuals and to enforce the data subject rights.

Judicial independence, particularly, is a **critical pillar** of such evaluations. The Commission examines whether individuals in the third country have **effective means of redress**, including access to independent courts and tribunals. The idea and concept of an effective remedy before an impartial tribunal stems from the EU Charter of Fundamental Rights to ensure that laws and courts are equipped to grant data subjects enforceable rights, including access, rectification, erasure, and redress.

2. Independent Supervisory Authority – The presence of an independent and functioning supervisory body with adequate powers and authorities is pivotal to investigating personal data breaches and intervening in any malpractices vis-à-vis personal data processing. The authority must have the power to penalize and impose sanctions.

Such supervisory authorities are expected to operate as a watchdog within the jurisdiction to also ensure compliance with the data protection laws and handle data subject complaints.

Another key aspect that is considered critical to the functioning of an independent supervisory authority is the cooperation with European authorities, particularly the EU Data Protection Board.

3. Adherence to International Commitments, Standards & Sectoral Laws – The adherence to international data protection guidelines and standards offers a broader context and assurances if the jurisdiction has taken a comprehensive approach to abide by the personal data protection principles. It helps the commission to determine if there is widespread adoption of established norms and standards like OECD Privacy guidelines or other voluntary standards, which is a reflection of global alignment and support for enforcement.

The adherence to international agreements and standards projects a consistent approach rather than an arbitrary adoption of personal protection. It helps to identify if the country respects data protection in trade agreements.

The adherence to international commitments enables the authorities to coordinate and cooperate in investigations and mutual legal assistance, which is extremely beneficial for the protection of rights associated with the data subjects.

The presence of sectoral law is equally important as it offers tailored legislation to handle sensitive personal data in fields like health and financial sectors, etc.

4. Access by Public Authorities – It is deemed an important factor because the unlawful or easy access to personal data without any transparent judicial process could enable the public authorities to have easier access to the personal data, making them victims of disproportionate surveillance.

This factor became more pronounced post-**Schrems II** as the concerns were heightened regarding U.S. surveillance practices.

Option 2. Use of Standard Contractual Clauses (SCCs) / Model Clauses

Standard contractual clauses are proposed controls in a lot of privacy laws and regulations. Therefore, they can be adopted to legally bind the organizations processing data outside jurisdictions. Some jurisdictions have also laid out the structure and language of the Standard contractual clauses therefore, it would be beneficial to look into those pre-approved contractual clauses.

Option 3. Binding Corporate Rules (BCRs)

Binding Corporate Rules act as safeguards that are beneficial for multinational entities and ensure that the various chapters or regional offices will adhere to **BCRs** as internal rules for personal data protection.

The Binding Corporate Rules must include enforceable data subject rights and accountability mechanisms.

Option 4. Conduct Transfer Impact Assessments (TIAs)

Transfer Impact Assessment (TIA) is a risk-based approach to identify and assess the risks associated with the transfer of personal data to a jurisdiction that is not on the adequacy list issued by the supervisory authority.

EU – GDPR particularly emphasizes the need to perform a transfer impact assessment particularly relying on the appropriate safeguards expressed within Article 46 of the EU-GDPR.

Its overarching purpose is to **verify and document** that the level of protection your data will enjoy abroad remains essentially equivalent to that guaranteed by the GDPR—and, if not, to identify what extra measures you must take.

The Privacy professionals must examine the following as part of their Transfer Impact Assessment exercise.

1. **Identify & document the Data Transfer details**
   o What data is being transferred?
   o To which party is data being transferred?
   o Map the Data flow.
   o What is the purpose behind the transfer of personal data?
   o Does the recipient have an effective Privacy program in place?

2. **Assess Safeguards' Effectiveness**
   o Are Standard contractual clauses or BCRs aligned with local laws?
   o Do local laws have provisions aligned with personal data protection principles? When the local laws demand submission of personal data or if the local laws carry an overriding power over your contract, then the safeguards will become irrelevant.
   o Can data subject rights be enforced?
   o Are there any surveillance risks that may harm the rights and freedoms of individuals?

3. **Propose administrative & technical controls.**
   o Encryption, pseudonymization, strict access controls, and contractual agreements.
   o Maintain Records and Update Privacy Notices.
   o Sign a data processing agreement (DPA) ensuring compliance with applicable laws.
   o Vendor risk assessments

4. **Decide, Explain & Document**

Once a TIA exercise is carried out, then the data privacy unit must propose the approach along with the rationale either to proceed with the transfer, require the other party to update or enhance the controls, or to choose a different service provider or a hosting provider.

Option 5. Explicit Consent of the Data Subject

Some privacy laws and regulations do leave it to the discretion of the individual to transfer the personal data beyond jurisdiction if no other safeguards are viable. However, this is also deemed as a last resort control. Therefore, the consent must be valid, explicitly obtained after allowing the individual to exercise an informed choice.

Option 6. Derogations & Certification Mechanisms

Some regulatory or supervisory authorities have also nominated bodies to examine and certify the adherence to the personal data protection mechanism adopted by the organizations. Such certification mechanisms can also be used to facilitate transfers of personal data beyond a jurisdiction.

EU – GDPR Article 49 offers another option termed as Derogations, which opens the door for personal data transfers beyond Europe only for exception and narrow scenarios. Such transfers are deemed necessary for the performance of a contract, public interest, legal claims, or vital interests of the data subjects.

Conclusion

Cross-border data transfers have become an undeniable business reality due to technological progress, increased globalization, and better trade integration among nations.

As data traverses across jurisdictions, the data privacy professionals have to understand and navigate a complex terrain shaped by privacy laws and regulations and geopolitical dynamics.

The approach put forward within the EU - GDPR — which is driven by adequacy decisions, appropriate safeguards, and the transfer impact assessment (TIA) has become a gold standard to be adopted and reflected in other laws to facilitate data transfers. The underlying principle behind the personal data transfer regulations is that the data and its associated subjects must enjoy the same level of protection as their originating jurisdiction as the data traverses across various jurisdictions.

The Data Privacy professionals must be wary of the fact that the personal data transfer regulations are not meant to prohibit the movement of personal data but to ensure that the transfer of personal data does not come at the expense of individuals' privacy, dignity, and freedoms.

3.3 Privacy Incident and Breach Management

All Privacy laws and regulations have a consistent theme to ensure that the individuals/data subjects are notified about the breach within a certain reasonable timeframe from the declaration of the breach. This consistent prominence stems from the understanding that individuals are likely to be a recipient of some tangible or intangible harm after a personal data breach has occurred.

It therefore gains substantial importance where an organisation must have an established and approved mechanism through which they can perform qualifications of purported breach and notify the individuals subsequently.

It is critical to create a mechanism or an operational framework that differentiates between an incident and a Breach. Ironically, the regulations often fail to create a distinction between the incident and breach, which leads to improper judgment, qualification, and distillation of facts.

Failing to distinguish between an incident and a breach can have grave consequences for the organizations whereby the insecure handling of personal data by employees that has not impacted the privacy of the individuals may be categorized as breach, thus forcing themselves to notify the individuals about the benign incident which have not necessarily left an adverse impact on the lives of the individuals. However, it's important to treat it as an incident and find the root causes behind the insecure handling of such data and ascertain if a Secure handling policy and procedure ever existed to handle the data in the case mentioned above. Failure to adequately analyse the root cause of an incident makes the organization rife with circumstances that will eventually cause a Privacy Breach.

Any mishandling of personal data by employees or vendors of the organization that does not result in tangible or intangible harm to the data subjects must be handled as an Incident, as the organizations always have institutional mechanisms, like internal policies, that facilitate taking punitive actions against such actions, whether of a collective or individual nature.

Before we dwell upon establishing a Privacy Incident and Breach Management framework, it is pivotal to differentiate between a Problem, Event, Incident, and Breach because the incorrect qualifications have immense ramifications that must be accounted for when establishing a Privacy Incident and Breach Management framework.

NOMENCLATURE	DESCRIPTION & EXAMPLES	RAMIFICATIONS
EVENT	Any occurrence or activity that is likely to have a positive or negative impact on the organization or individuals. Events are supposed to be investigated before they culminate in a problem or an incident. **Example:** Security Operations Centre Team observing reconnaissance being performed on the information assets of the organization. Such events need to be investigated to determine if they are benign or malignant before declaring them as an incident based on observed impact.	If left unattended, then may lead to negative consequences in the form of a problem or an incident.
PROBLEM	An event that may cause discomfort or disruption with an impact that can be limited to specific individuals or spread across all organizations. A problem is always meant to have an adverse impact of varying severity levels. **Example:** An employee unable to log on to his machine because he/she forgot their password and thus unable to timely process payrolls, which require personal data.	If Problems are left unattended, then they may culminate in an Incident.
INCIDENT	Any unplanned interruption, disruption, or degradation of services that may be caused by different threat vectors. Incidents are likely to occur as a result of internal policy violations by the staff.	Poor Incident Management handling and poor root cause analysis debilitate the

	Example: An employee handling the data backups in an inappropriate manner, thus damaging the data, which is likely to impact the business revenue engine. **Example:** An employee storing the unencrypted files containing personal information on the shared folder is likely to affect the privacy of the individuals. **Example:** An HR employee divulging the salary information of a staff member to his/her colleagues. In all the above incident scenarios, the organizations have the leverage to take punitive and corrective actions against the offender.	organization from fixing the core issues, whereby external threat actorexternal threat actors can exploit such weakness can exploit such weakness to carry out a Breach.
BREACH	Any incident in which the external party breaches the fortress of controls or exploits the weakness in controls to adversely impact the personal data. A poorly designed control framework enables the threat actors to exploit the weakness in the organizational control framework. Therefore, a lack of or a weakness in any control does not constitute a policy violation.	Requires notification of the breach to the individuals. Penalties, fines, and reputation damage.

	Example: A threat actor penetrates the organizational network and encrypts the data on the databases for ransom.	
	Example: A threat actor exfiltrates the personal data and publishes it online for any kind of retribution.	
	Breaches do not occur overnight. They are an outcome of a prolonged series of control failures.	

When an organization fails to adequately unpack the reasons behind the occurrence of the incident and the manner in which an incident was handled, then they remain susceptible to similar kinds of events, and such events culminate in incidents, and the failure to bridge gaps identified during incident handling further facilitates the occurrence of a Privacy breach.

In the same breath, it is important to realize that there are often multiple other incident management frameworks operating within the organisation, either related to IT, Information Security, Business Continuity, and Operational Risk, as the regulations and standards relating to these disciplines also carry incident-specific pronouncements.

It therefore requires you to carve out a path through which the Privacy incidents and Breaches are clearly identified and acted upon. Failing to lay down the boundaries and identifying the tangents across the different incident management frameworks within an organization often leads to a chaotic situation where each function may occasionally step on each other's toes.

It may be a case where an incident could only be an IT incident but not necessarily a cybersecurity or a privacy incident, but there is also the likelihood that an incident may qualify to be an IT, Cybersecurity, and a Privacy incident at the same time.

Consider the malware outbreak that may impact the availability of your IT infrastructure, thus impacting the revenue engine of the organization. Since it relies on a cyber threat vector therefore it qualifies to be a cybersecurity and an IT incident as well. As a result of such a malware outbreak, if the personal data is exfiltrated or compromised, then it will qualify as a

Privacy breach as well. Aligning your framework with other incident management frameworks helps to correctly diagnose the spread of the issue and address it from respective ends.

The incident categorizations or classification help to determine if the identified event can even be qualified as an incident. If it is one, then can it be considered a Privacy incident or not? Once an incident is qualified to be a Privacy incident, then a Damage assessment must be performed to gauge the likelihood of any tangible or intangible harm to the data subjects.

Creating an incident categorization as below will always be helpful for an organization for effective qualification of the incidents and breaches.

PRIVACY INCIDENT CLASSIFICATION	
CLASSIFICATION	**DESCRIPTION**
Personal Data Loss or Exfiltration.	**Incident:** When organizational employees share, transfer, post outside, or damage any personal data in an unauthorized and uncontrolled manner by bypassing or subverting organizational controls. **Breach:** When a threat actor takes advantage by subverting organizational controls to transfer, leak, and/or post any personal data outside the organization.
Unauthorized Processing & Storage.	When organizational employees process, store personal information without appropriate approvals and implementation of adequate controls.
Unsolicited Personal Data Collection.	When organizational employees collect personal information from internal and/or external customers without due notification and adequate controls.
Unauthorized Personal Data Disclosure.	**Breach** When personal data is transferred/disclosed to any external parties without adequate approvals and authorizations as defined within the organizational policies.

Damage to Personal Data Integrity.	**Incident:** When organizational employees cause damage to the integrity of personal information owned by an organization, thus negatively affecting the business. **Breach:** When a threat actor takes advantage by subverting an organization's controls to damage the integrity of personal information.

Tying in the incident categories with the severity levels helps to further deal with the incidents in a more effective manner. However it is worth mentioning that severity levels are more beneficial for the organizational incident handling, even though they factor in a component for damage to the number of personal data records or individuals. While the laws do not see breaches in the context of thresholds, it is always beneficial to have a Privacy incident severity level that defines the thresholds. Some incident management regulations within the jurisdictions may compel the organizations to notify the regulators if an incident beyond a specific severity threshold materializes.

It therefore becomes significant that to establish a Damage assessment criterion within the organization that can facilitate the data privacy function to objectively assess the potential impact of an incident to the data subjects. If such an impact may cause harm to the rights, interests and freedoms of the individuals then they must be duly notified within the timelines identified within the applicable laws & regulations.

DAMAGE ASSESSMENT CRITERIA	
DIRECT DAMAGES	**INDIRECT DAMAGES**
1. **Identity Theft:** The leaked personal data can be exploited for identity theft, leading to financial fraud, unauthorized transactions, extortion, or blackmailing.	1. **Emotional Distress:** Personal data exposure causes fear, stress, and anxiety among individuals.
2. **Privacy Invasion:** Exposure of personal information may lead to unsolicited communication, threats, spam, or targeted advertising.	2. **Trust Issues:** Personal data exposure makes individuals more skeptical and cautious about sharing personal data in the future.

3. **Financial Loss:** Hackers gaining access to personal data, which may result in financial or monetary losses or unauthorized charges.	3. **Future Security Issues:** Leaked data can be used for future cybercrimes, increasing the risk of further privacy breaches or security incidents, and fraud attempts.
4. **Unfair Treatment:** Personal data exposure leading to unfair, biased, or discrimination treatment inflicted upon the individuals.	4. **Reputational Damage:** Data exposure harms the data subject's personal or professional reputation by causing any embarrassment.

The above damage assessment criteria are not exhaustive and are intended solely to assist organizations in objectively evaluating potential harm to individuals. It is important to note, however, that indirect damages should only be considered when a direct harm has materialized. Individuals may occasionally express disproportionate concerns—such as an unfounded fear of reputational harm- and may request information from the organization even when no actual or direct damage has occurred.This approach helps to strike a balance between the organizational interests with the rights, interests, and freedoms of the individuals.

Another key aspect of establishing a Privacy Incident and breach management framework is to establish cooperation mechanisms with other key stakeholders within the organization, such as the legal department, crisis management committee, and the crisis communication team.

Leveraging the support of the legal team can aid the organization in examining the potential damage to the individuals as a result of a breach and what legal commitments need to be honoured in such a case.

Crisis Management Committee usually comprises all the chief officers within the organization. Similarly, crisis communication is a function that resides under the Crisis Management Team. The data privacy division must establish points of engagement with the crisis management team to seek facilitation in cases of Breach notification to be sent to data subjects and the regulatory authority.

The data privacy division must set and manage expectations along with the secretary of the committee to pin down the circumstances in which the support of the committee will be required, what information will be fed to the committee in what time frame, and what actions and approvals will be expected from the committee.

Marking out such tangents within the privacy incident and breach management framework is a critical aspect to demonstrate an organization's commitment to uphold and protect the individual's rights, interests, and freedoms so that in case of a privacy breach, the individuals are notified prior to suffering harm or damage.

In most cases, the crisis communication team will facilitate the communication of a breach to the individuals and the regulatory authorities. The data privacy teams must understand the minimum information that must be communicated to the individuals and the regulatory authorities.

The crisis communication team can develop sample texts to be communicated, incorporating the minimum information sets to be provided by the data privacy. This helps to minimize the time taken to brainstorm about the *text of the message. In the same* breadth, the data privacy division must work with the crisis communication team to identify the potential channels through which the individuals must be working.

Establishing such cooperation mechanisms is not just helpful in increasing the effectiveness of the Privacy incident and breach management framework. Still, they also serve as evidence to demonstrate compliance and due diligence institutionalized within the organization.

Awareness of the Privacy Incident & Breach Management framework:

Conducting awareness of privacy incident and breach management framework is another key component to exhibiting due diligence and commitment to upholding the rights, interests, and freedoms of individuals.

Once a Privacy incident and breach management framework is established, then it must be well understood by the employees and staff of the organisation. The data privacy division must identify correct channels, like email flyers, electronic screens within the organization, or auditoriums, to conduct different kinds of awareness.

Email flyers and electronic screens can be leveraged to provide crisp information about what constitutes a breach and what the different categories of incidents are identified within the organizational privacy incident and breach management framework.

The employees must be made aware and informed about any of the activities that could lead to a privacy breach and subject them to employment violations. Therefore, the precise awareness campaigns must brief them about what is meant by each privacy incident category and how to avoid them. Workshops must be conducted to unpack every layer of the privacy incident management framework. However, considering the audience of the workshop, the details of the discussion may need to be tailored. For example, if the workshop attendees are all the C-level executives of the organization, then only explaining the contours of the privacy incident and breach, along with penalties and regulatory requirements, can be covered.

However, the senior managers and the underlying teams must be educated about the detailed aspects of the framework to ensure that the framework is effectively implemented within the organisation.

Tabletop exercises can be arranged with different stakeholders of the organization to assess the readiness of the teams with regard to the understanding of their roles and responsibilities.

Performing Root Cause Analysis & Recording Incidents & Breaches:

Documenting root cause analysis exhibits an act of due diligence by the organization that has suffered a breach. However, it is equally important that the root cause analysis must capture correct facts correlating with the occurrence of the breach.

One question that may surface during the root cause analysis would be the impact of the breach on the organization. However, quantifying the impact of the personal data breach is not often that easy because the quantification requires examination of below factors.

1. Direct Cost – It can be calculated by multiplying the number of hours for which the services were impacted by the revenue made by organizations per hour. Hence, the organization generates a revenue of X US dollars, and if the services were impacted so one can conclude the direct cost to be $3 \times X = 3X$.

Another aspect of the direct cost is the penalties and fines imposed by the regulator in handling of a data breach.

2. Indirect Cost/Clean-up Cost – As a result of a personal data breach, the organisation may uncover the lack of some technological solution that could aid in either preventing the breach or detecting it earlier. Regulators may compel the organizations on occasion to implement specific technological solutions, and with each such solution comes a licensing cost, professional services cost, computational cost, and the human resources cost.

3. Reputational Cost – While the previous two costs are easier to quantify but the reputational cost calculation is not easier to measure. An organization may have recovered from the breach, provided all the necessary remedies to the individuals, and yet may be subject to some fears lurking in the minds of its customers. This is often expressed in the gradual churn-out of the users, while the organization may have up-scaled their marketing and advertising efforts, yet yielding no significant results in favour of the organization.

It is therefore important for the data privacy professionals to set the expectations of the management stakeholders from the early stages about the potential consequences of the breach.

The root cause analysis must be signed by the important stakeholders from the organisation, like the data management team, the privacy team, the information security team, IT, and the senior management team. Documentation of and signatures upon the root cause analysis is the affirmation to the fact that the organizational stakeholders agree to the underlying causes that led to the privacy incident or the breach, and hence a corrective action plan is necessary to prevent such occurrences in the future.

3.4 Data Retention & Disposal.

Data retention is a critical concept that supports the principle of storage limitation by ensuring personal data is not kept longer than necessary. In essence, data retention refers to the continued storage of personal data within an organization's ICT infrastructure for business or operational purposes. However, many technical terms and classifications established before the advent of modern privacy regulations often fail to reflect the true intent of data protection principles. As a result, the industry has come to treat data archiving as a separate concept from data retention, despite both involving the storage of information. It is important to recognize that archiving is, in fact, a form of retention and should be treated as such within privacy frameworks.

The differentiation created using nomenclatures as Data Retention & Archiving, divorces the fact that in both scenarios, the act of data storage continues to take place. Therefore, if an organization has moved the data from Retention infrastructure (Online environment) to an alternative environment deemed as Archived data, that does not eliminate the risks of personal data exposure or unauthorized processing or storage. Any data therefore stored (retained) in any environment without any legal basis is therefore deemed unlawful and violates the personal data protection principle of Storage Limitation.

It is therefore being proposed here that Data Retention should be deemed as online & archival storage of the data into separate infrastructure components. The online data is the warm or hot data on which the revenue stream is dependent. If this data is impacted, it will adversely affect the organization's ability to create value and also the data subjects.

However, the archived data is the refrigerated data or cold storage data on which the business revenue stream is not dependent. Still, such data needs to be retained either for fraud or other investigation purposes. Additionally, if such personal data is also exposed or compromised, then it may bring about adverse consequences for the data subjects.

It is pivotal for privacy professionals to understand that the data must be disposed of at the conclusion of the data lifecycle, and failure to establish a mechanism that ensures timely and secure disposal of personal data is akin to mis commitment to the individuals and also a violation of the privacy laws and regulations. The DPOs can work with the database administrators and the other IT infrastructure experts to ensure that information systems contain scripts or stored procedures that are capable of disposing of the personal data at the conclusion of the data lifecycle.

It is also important to be able to distinguish between the Media disposal and the data disposal activities. Media is a term that can be associated with backup tapes, hard drives, and other forms of storage. When the media has completed its life and needs to be disposed of, then it must be cleansed of any data residing in the media using secure disposal standards.

However, there are scenarios when the media may not be end-of-life. In that case, the data housed in the media may have completed its retention age. Therefore, in such circumstances, only the data needs to be securely disposed of without disposing of the media.

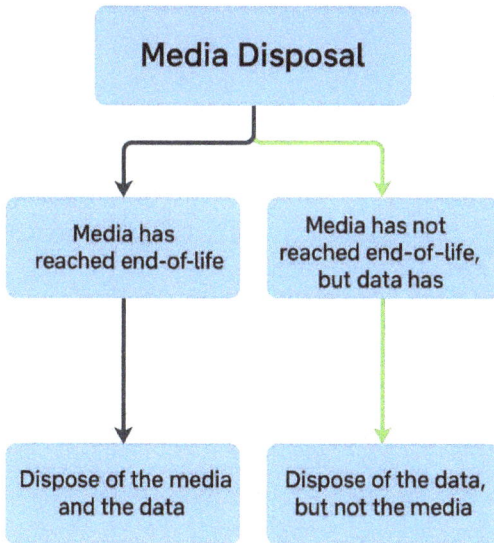

Let's take a hypothetical scenario to unpack the constituents of the Storage Limitation principle and see how the principle of Storage Limitation can be applied in practice.

Consider a hypothetical product named "Financial Risk Indulgence Score" that provides a score to the credit card companies for the consumers who utilize the credit card. The company develops an underlying algorithm that will calculate the risk score, and it requires a maximum of 3 years of personal spending records to generate a credible risk score. Additionally, the credit card companies are also mandated to maintain consumer spending records for up to 5 years through a regulatory instrument.

Taking into account the above requirements, the retention period (including archive) can be considered as 5 years and it can be broken down into the following manner.

Driver For Data Retention/Storage	Period
Business Obligations	Maximum of 3 years.
Regulatory Requirement	Maximum of 5 years.

The above business requirements must be translated into the IT design to ensure that business, regulatory requirements are fulfilled along with the principle of storage limitation.

DATA LIFECYCLE STAGES		
ONLINE ENVIRONMENT	ARCHIVED ENVIRONMENT	DISPOSAL
(Latest Data up to 3 years) **HOT DATA**	(Any Data which is older than 3 years but not older than 5 years) **COLD DATA**	Any data that is older than 5 years from its inception must be disposed of.

BENEFITS OF THE ABOVE PROPOSED APPROACH

Designing the Retention scheme of personal data in the above proposed manner has the following benefits:

1. BETTER BUSINESS RESILIENCE:

Since the data stored in an online environment is hot/warm data on which the business revenue stream is dependent, in case of a crisis or business outage, it is always easier to restore the data, which is smaller in size. In the above example, restoring the 3-year data from backup requires less time than restoring 5 years of personal data.

This ensures that the personal data is easily available for use or for providing services to the customers.

2. REDUCING RISK OF PERSONAL DATA EXPOSURE

When an organization splits and segregates the storage/retention of personal data into two separate environments as Online or archive, it mitigates the risk of personal data exposure. The storage of all personal data without any regard for the hot/cold data nature centralizes the data. Therefore, a threat actor has a single source to compromise and lay their hands on a bigger chunk of personal data.

Also, by segregating the personal data into online and archived environments and implementing the principles of segregation of duties you can further reduce the risk surface where individuals who manage the infrastructure containing online data should be prevented from accessing the cold data contained in archived environment or there can be administrative procedures created to ensure that cross referencing of personal data is controlled and driven only by a lawful purpose.

When the personal data is physically, logically, or administratively segregated, then it creates more hurdles for the threat actors to lay their hands on the personal data of the individual

3. OPERATIONAL EFFICIENCY

The online data requires more rigorous and frequent backups since the changes to such data are more frequent than the data that needs to be archived. An organization may avail the luxury of taking backups for archived data on a much lesser frequency since the delta will be smaller. Thus reducing the human effort and computational cycles.

It is important to reiterate here that the data retention period identified within the Privacy notice is a commitment towards the individuals/data subjects, and hence, the personal data must be securely disposed of at the end of the retention period. If the personal data is not securely disposed of at the conclusion of the retention period, then it defies the essence of the storage limitation principle and compromises on the rights of the individuals.

If the organization wishes to retain the personal data indefinitely, then it must be guarded by a sound legal basis, or such personal data must be safeguarded through adequate controls.

3.5 Consent Management.

Consent solicitation is the first and foremost idea that comes to the minds of individuals whenever they believe that their rights and freedoms are being impinged upon. An individual may not necessarily use the privacy lexicon to express his/her desire or concerns around consent, but the idea is universally accepted and understood. It is therefore pivotal for privacy professionals to understand the underpinnings behind the consent.

Consent embodies the principle to allow individuals their moral and fundamental right to govern their private affairs, where they are equipped to and allowed to make informed and voluntary decisions about their lives.

As we stated earlier in the book, data has become the commodity to be exchanged and processed to create value. Therefore, the individuals to whom that data point are also likely to be treated as mere commodities rather than subjects with fundamental human rights.

The various personal data points elements linked to an individual provide details about an individual's life and choices that they exercise and therefore their personal choices are likely to be used in their favor or against them.

The famous philosopher Immanuel Kant professed the principle of treating individuals as end and not as means to ends. Consent is therefore a fundamental pillar in personal data protection that helps to determine the legal and ethical roots behind the processing of personal data.

Consent solicitation and revocation are ethical safeguards to regulate the equilibrium between the big organizations and the individuals whose data is being processed, and they tie in with the personal data protection principle of transparency and fairness discussed earlier. The below section unpacks the critical constituents of consent as determined by the EU-GDPR to ensure that individuals are prevented from exploitation and are provided with meaningful choices and options for remedy.

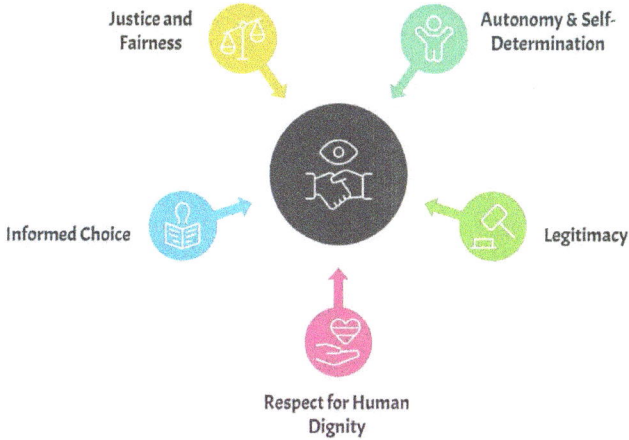

Figure 21 - Moral Roots for Consent Management

Consent is one of the lawful purposes that remains consistent in all the privacy regulatory instruments to ensure that individuals are given avenues to exercise a meaningful, informed, and voluntary choice and decide upon an option.

However, the data privacy professionals must guard against a firewall placed between consent and a legal obligation as two separate lawful purposes. It is important to understand the reasons why consent cannot be deemed as the sole lawful purpose and why there is a need for a legal obligation as a lawful purpose.

In cases where the collective interests of society are at stake, they often need to be upheld by virtue of the law or regulation because the absence of the law or regulation would essentially jeopardize the collective interests of society. However, in such cases, the subjected law needs to ensure that it has adequate provisions to uphold the rights, interests, and freedoms of individuals vis-à-vis Privacy.

In cases where the interests of the individual are at stake without compromising the collective interests of society, consent is used as a tool to shift power back to the individual to choose the data that identifies them.

This firewall between the different lawful purposes within Privacy is an important component in striking a balance between the competing interests within societies.

187

Principles of Effective Consent Management

Below are a few principles that must be considered while designing the consent management panel for your organizational services. The DPOs must be able to review, validate, and approve the panel's front and backend capabilities to ensure that the DPOs attest to the fact that privacy by design requirements were fulfilled in the development of consent management panels.

1. Transparency and Openness:

Consent must be obtained by presenting information upfront in plain and easy-to-understand language. The data subjects must be served with a privacy notice that can be layered, presenting summaries upfront with links to detailed information. The users must be prompted based on the context as they are about to engage with features or services that would require the collection of their personal data.

2. Granularity

The Data Privacy professionals must work with the application design team to ensure that if multiple personal data processing activities are linked to consent, then it must not be bundled into a single blanket consent.

Consent solicitation must be tied to the specific purpose of personal data processing, giving individuals the liberty and their right to allow types of personal data collection and processing while rejecting others.

Figure 22 - Consent Panel with Granular Options

188

3. Unambiguous Indication and Explicit Consent

Valid consent demands an avenue through which the users exercise an affirmative choice through the selection of an option or a tick-box. This means that the users must opt in to the personal data processing activities rather than having an option to opt out.

Privacy professionals must refer to their privacy regulations and their requirements with regard to explicit consent, as not all personal data processing activities may necessarily require explicit consent. Certain privacy laws and regulations leave the room open for implicit consent. In such cases, the individuals must be provided with easy access to means through which they can opt out.

Users should not be coerced into providing consent as a condition for accessing a service unless the data is strictly necessary.

4. Consent Revocation.

The DPOs and the privacy professionals must exercise caution in deciding whether Consent serves as the most appropriate lawful purpose of processing because consent is often easier to solicit. Still, most privacy laws require that the individuals must be equipped with the choice and avenue to revoke the consent.

Consent revocation must be ideally enabled through similar means as those through which consent was obtained, or they must be as easy as the avenue for consent solicitation.

Preference centers or dashboards enable effective withdrawal and update of choices. It is necessary to maintain the logs and the backend records of the timestamp when the user revoked the consent.

The toggle options can be adopted within the consent panel design to ensure that individuals can revoke the consent. Whenever the consent is withdrawn, the relevant logs must be maintained at the backend.

5. Consent Lifecycle Management

The DPOs and the privacy professionals must link the data lifecycle with the consent lifecycle. In certain circumstances, the personal data is collected multiple times due to the efficacy of the processing and because the previously collected data may not serve the purpose.

It is often seen in the medical sector when blood samples may need to be obtained from the patient or the beneficiary of services for carrying out medical tests. While the hospital or the medical care providers may have obtained consent from the same person earlier but with every collection and the nature of tests to be carried out, the purpose of processing associated with the nature of medical tests is changing. In such cases, the previously obtained consent may not work and therefore requires obtaining a new consent.

Similarly, the data lifecycle is tied to the data retention period, and consent is only valid till the data retention period expires. The organizations are expected to securely dispose of personal data once the data lifecycle expires. If an organization fails to securely dispose of personal data after the retention period expires, then the previously solicited consent will no longer make such personal data processing lawful.

It is therefore important to link consent with the data lifecycle and ensure that it is tracked throughout its lifecycle. It must be obtained again when processing purposes change, new data is collected, or legal requirements are updated.

6. Consent Channels

Consent channels are extremely important to protect the rights of the data subjects, but also to ensure that organizations have audit logs to demonstrate that consent was provided by the data subjects.

Channels that do not offer non-repudiation are not ideal for obtaining consent because consent may be held questionable because of the repudiation concerns.

When a data subject decides to take an action relating to consent, they are supposed to be provided with the privacy notice or the link to the privacy notice. However, if the channel does not have the capacity to present the privacy notice, then it may not be the most appropriate channel for consent solicitation.

Below are a few proposed channels and interfaces that are beneficial for organizations and data subjects as well.

1. Web-based Interfaces

Cookie banners, web forms, and layered privacy notices are common methods. They must allow genuine choice and be designed to minimize manipulation (e.g., avoiding dark patterns).

2. Mobile Applications

Mobile apps should use OS-level permission dialogs supplemented with in-app explanations. Features should request permission when needed ("just-in-time" consent).

3. IVRs, IoT, and Limited-UI Devices

Devices with minimal interfaces may use companion apps, QR codes, or audio cues to deliver consent information and capture decisions.

7. Consent Recording and Auditability

It is necessary for privacy professionals to understand that these consent logs have a legal value, and in cases where the data subject questions the validity of consent, these logs will serve to prove that consent was provided.

The design of the logic through which consent records will be maintained must be reviewed and approved by the DPO to ensure that the logic fulfills the privacy requirements and that all relevant metadata is incorporated.

Consent should be stored as structured data with appropriate metadata like User ID, timestamp, Privacy Notice version, consent status, and processing purposes. It is essential that consent records carry a linkage to user or session identifiers.

The DPOs and privacy professionals must pull up a sample of consent logs on a periodic basis to ensure that consent records are being maintained in accordance with the logic.

Conclusion

An effective consent management approach goes beyond legal and regulatory compliance, ensuring and demonstrating commitment to data subjects' right to choice, autonomy, and transparency.

The DPOs must bridge the ethical and operational elements associated with consent. It is equally important to guard against deceptive or coercive manners to obtain consent because it erodes the trust in the minds of the individuals towards the products and the services offered by the organization.

3.6 Operationalizing Data Subject Rights

Data Subjects are a common theme in various privacy laws and regulations, often expressed either in similar or in different lexicons. The handling of data subject requests can be resource-intensive and an exhaustive exercise for organizations, as it is the only functional requirement within the realm of personal data protection with which a specific timeline is associated, compelling organizations to ensure that the requests are processed within 30 days or whatever is expressed in the relevant privacy laws and regulations.

This section is developed to provide broad-based guidance for the DPOs to establish governance and operations for effective dispensation of data subject rights. The section does not delve into examining each data subject's right, but delves into examining the data subject requests at the following three layers:

Mental Map for Handling Data Subject Requests.

Whenever data subject requests are raised to the DPO, it requires a careful understanding and examination of the requests raised by the individuals. Most of the jurisdictions already have various consumer protection laws and regulations that have been established to offer protection to consumer rights and avenues for seeking remedies. It is therefore important to understand the convergence and divergence between the data subject rights and the consumer protection rights.

This section offers a mental map to the privacy professionals to clearly examine and act upon the data subject requests:

Step 1. DOES THE REQUEST FALL UNDER THE DATA SUBJECT RIGHTS, OR IS IT A GENERAL CONSUMER COMPLAINT?

The data subjects may often raise requests that do not fall under a data subject request. The privacy professionals need to recognize the industrial sector in which they operate and the clientele of their organization. For example, the banks and hospitals are considered sensitive, and often the individuals (data subjects) may be yearning for immediate help and remedy, and making distress calls to organizations and thereby use the touchpoints which are created by the organization to handle data subject requests.

Privacy professionals and the DPOs must be able to distinguish between a data subject request and a conventional customer complaint that can include any of the following non-exhaustive cases:

- Inability to log in to the portal or mobile application.
- Unable to receive one-time password for authentication.
- Unauthorized transaction on a credit or debit card.
- Inability to reserve appointments in hotels, restaurants, or hospitals, etc.
- Issues about the quality of services and disruptions within the services.

It is important to recognize that all data subjects may not be exercising their rights under the tag line of data subject requests and may not have a nuanced understanding of the privacy laws and regulations. The individuals are expected to raise the data subjects in an expression suited to them; therefore, the privacy professional must be able to recognize and identify the following categories (*non-exhaustive*) of the requests that can fall under the data subject requests:

- Inquiry about the collection and processing of personal data.
- I request that to delete my data held and processed by your organization.

- My data in the possession of your organization is not correct or updated. I'm seeking support to update my personal data.
- I'm requesting access to my personal data held and processed by your organization.
- The latest e-statement of my bank account does not contain correct information. I'm requesting to correct the information.
- I've concerns over the working mechanism of your algorithms, therefore I do not want my personal data to be processed in an automated manner.
- I've already settled my university dues, but my profile still shows an overdue payment, which I would like to have checked and corrected.

Some of the examples as mentioned above are often handled under the consumer protection rights as well; therefore, the data privacy unit must align with the customer care division to understand the nature of complaints received by them and if they have an operational mechanism capable of providing remedies to such requests. The cases in which the organization has already established an operational and effective mechanism to offer remedies related to personal data correction or processing, the data privacy unit must ensure that such requests are first routed to the customer care division.

The cases in which the organization has not created an avenue for treating data subject requests must be picked up by the data privacy team for further perusal from their end. In some cases, the data subject may have failed to get the required remedy from customer care relating to personal data processing and the data subject may have opted to reach out to data privacy for a remedy as a last resort.

The DPO and the privacy professionals must ensure that such cases are effectively looked after to provide an effective and efficient solution. The DPOs may escalate such cases to customer care units internally for expedited response.

Step 2.   IDENTIFY THE NATURE OF DATA SUBJECT REQUESTS.

Once the data privacy team has determined the requests to be a legitimate data subject request, it is important to identify the nature of the right being exercised by the individual because the subsequent analysis and response will significantly depend on the nature of the data subject requests:

Types of Data Subject rights: *(non-exhaustive and may vary subject to different regulations)*

1. *Right to be informed.*
2. *Right of access by the data subject.*
3. *Right to correction or rectification.*
4. *Right to request erasure or deletion.*

5. *Right to restriction of processing.*
6. *Right to object.*

Step 3.   DETERMINE THE RELATIONSHIP BETWEEN THE DATA SUBJECT AND THE ORGANIZATION.
The next step is to determine the nature of the relationship between the data subject and the organization. The data subject can be a consumer of the organizational services, a customer, an employee or a third-party consultant. In some cases, the individual may be exercising the data subject rights on behalf of a deceased person who happened to be the actual data subject. Therefore, the relationship of the data subject with the organization is critical to appropriately analyze the data subject request and to later approve or deny the request with an explanation.

Step 4.   EXAMINE IF THE ORGANIZATION COLLECTED THE DATA DIRECTLY FROM THE DATA SUBJECT OR NOT.
Once the relationship of the data subject is identified with the organization, then it is equally important to determine whether the organization has collected the data directly from the individual or if is it being processed due to an onward transfer. This is extremely important in scenarios where the organization is obligated by the regulatory authorities to collect and process PII from a particular authority, and therefore dispensation of data subject rights may pose a challenge that needs to be navigated carefully by the DPOs.

Step 5.   DETERMINE THE LEGAL BASIS FOR PERSONAL DATA PROCESSING.
Determine the lawful purpose for processing personal data. This becomes particularly important when the data subjects wish to exercise their right to erasure, rectification, and object to processing. In cases of legal obligation, the organization may not have the luxury to dispense the right if other laws and regulations prohibit so.

It must be noted that consent is the most suitable legal basis for individuals and the most restrictive legal basis for organizations. On the contrary, the legal obligation is the most suitable legal basis for the organizations and the most restrictive legal basis for the individuals because in the presence of a legal obligation, the organizations are obligated to collect and process personal data within the boundaries of associated law or a regulation.

Step 6.   EXAMINE THE ROLE OF THE ORGANIZATION IN PERSONAL DATA PROCESSING.
Determine if your organization is involved in the processing as a controller or a processor. If your organization is involved in the processing as a Data processor, then the above validations and analysis must be carried out in accordance with the guidelines of the data controller.

In cases of joint controllers, the organizations involved in joint processing must determine how the data subject rights will be dispensed.

Step 7. ACCEPTANCE OR DENY REQUESTS WITH AN EXPLANATION.

Once the above factors and steps have been carried out, the privacy professionals in the data privacy unit must decide whether to accept the data subject request or to deny the request. If the request is denied, then it must be accompanied by a justifiable and clear explanation to the data subjects.

If the request is accepted, then it must be notified to the data subjects or the requestor along with the expected timelines to complete the processing of the request.

Establishing Backbone for Operationalizing Data Subject Access Requests Handling

The efficient dispensation of data subject rights is significantly dependent on a refined procedure for handling data subject requests, the technological infrastructure capable of handling such requests at scale, and a clear mental map through which the data privacy unit will act upon the requests raised by the data subjects. This section is geared towards helping the DPOs to construct a procedural mechanism and the technological infrastructure that is pivotal for sustainable data subject requests handling.

Step 1. DATA SUBJECTS TOUCH POINT WITH THE ORGANIZATION.

To enable individuals to exercise their rights vis-à-vis their personal data, it is fundamental to create a touchpoint through which individuals can exercise their rights. The Privacy notice is a well-established channel adopted by organizations within which data protection officers' email addresses can be provided.

Additionally, a link or a form can be added to the organizational website that collects the following information from the data subjects when they raise a Data subject request:

Table 12 Proposed Fields to be collected in DSR.

FIELDS	DESCRIPTION & PURPOSE
Name of the Data Subject	Name of the individual having a relationship with the organization.
Contact Number *(for correspondence)*	These fields can also be used to perform authentication of the data subject through one-time passwords.
Email *(for correspondence)*	

ID Information *(if applicable)*	May include national IDs or passport information against which individuals' data is linked.
Request Type	There can be a drop-down or a check box to allow the individuals to exercise the relevant rights.
Relationship with the Organization	<ul><li>Consumer/Client/Customer.</li><li>Employee.</li><li>Vendor or Third Party.</li><li>Others.</li></ul>
Free Text Field	An additional text field can be provided to the data subject to share an elaborate expression of their request.

Once the individual submits the form, there can be a pop-up notification issued to the data subject to brief them about the timelines associated with handling of the requests. The timelines communicated to the data subjects must be in accordance with the privacy laws and regulations incumbent upon the organization.

In case the data subjects wish to exercise their right to be informed about the personal data processing, then there is no need to perform authentication of the user. Such scenarios require a simple pop-up notification to redirect data subjects towards the privacy notice.

Once the individual has submitted the data subject requests, it must be logged into the database with relevant details such as the Data subject ID, the Nature of the requests, and time of the request submission.

Such logging is essential for demonstrating compliance and also to ensure efficient handling of data subject requests.

Step 2. REQUEST ANALYSIS.

Once the data request has been logged into the system, it needs to be handled by the data privacy team by following the above-mentioned steps expressed in the section of Mental Map for Handling Data Subject Requests.

This step will help to determine whether the request of the data subject is to be accepted or denied. If the request for access to personal data is processed, then there must be a technological mechanism established to enable the data privacy team to perform the following steps:

Reporting Data Subject Requests Metrics and KPIs.

The DPO must ensure that there is effective reporting for the handling of data subject requests to senior management. This can be done by collecting the data from the system that logs all the data subject requests. Such reporting is essential to ensure continual improvement of the data subjects' rights handling.

The following data elements can be used to carry out effective reporting for data subjects' rights:

- Number of data subjects requests handled in a month.
- Breakdown of the categories of requests handled in a month. This should showcase the number of access rights exercised, the number of erasure requests processed, etc.
- Number of requests handled within the SLA.

These reports must also identify the challenges related to data subject requests handling, the management needs to assess if the challenges can be addressed through better allocation of resources, re-engineering the procedures, or adoption of technology.

3.7 Data Controllers & Processors – Governance, Power Asymmetry & Price of Error.

The idea of data controllers and processors is pivotal to determining the responsibilities and accountabilities between the parties involved in the processing of personal data. While this demarcation and identification of roles appear trivial and easy, they carries enormous implications on the parties involved in personal data processing. The appropriate definition of roles, responsibilities, and accountabilities is crucial as this sets in motion the responsibilities for implementation of privacy controls like dispensation of privacy notices, data subject rights, consent solicitation, ultimate accountability for compliance, etc.

If these roles are not determined with adequate application of mind, due diligence, and boundaries expressed within the European Data Protection guidelines for concepts of controllers and processors, then the first casualty of misclassification is the data subjects, as their expectations around receiving privacy notice, dispensation of data subject rights may not be fulfilled.

The latter and deeper casualty is the business where an organization may unnecessarily embrace or abandon responsibility compliance. Such misidentification may eventually lead to cost overruns or penalties from regulators for poorly identifying their role in personal data processing.

This chapter is written to bring prominence to such scenarios where the apparent and simple understandings of controller and processor may be deceptive and require a more nuanced and deeper inspection of business arrangement, service level agreements, and the data flows between various parties and the acts of processing at each end.

Before we delve into discussing complex scenarios related to Data Controllers and Processors, it is important to refresh the definitions and the understanding of Data Controllers and Processors pronounced in EDPB's Guidelines 07/2020 on the concepts of controller and processors. It is important to keep in mind that other privacy laws and regulations that have similar underpinnings as EU-GDPR carry the same tone to express the idea of data controllers and processors.

Data Controllers - "The natural or legal person, public authority, agency or other body which, alone or jointly with others, determines the purposes and means of the processing of personal data".

EDPB lays out the five foundational blocks necessary to qualify for a data controller, which are given below. This section will shed light on two of the most important components that are critical for DPOs to understand to make a correct determination about the Data controller and the processor.

1. Natural or legal person, public authority, agency, or other body.
2. Determines.
3. Alone or jointly with others.
4. Purposes and means.
5. Personal Data Processing.

From the above foundational blocks, the second block of **"determines"** is a very powerful block that sheds light on the power and influence exercised by the controller to decide around key elements of personal data processing. Due to this ability of the controller to influence key decisions around personal data processing, the controllers are ultimately accountable for personal data processing.

The EDPB guidelines point to two major categories through which the controllers are able to exercise the power of determining the purpose of processing:

1. Control Stemming from Legal Provisions – This is the scenario where a specific organization or public bodies may be entrusted or authorized to collect and process specific personal data by virtue of some other regulations within the jurisdictional boundaries. These scenarios are often straightforward as there are explicit legal provisions that empower the organization to collect such personal data. Determining the controllers in such circumstances is an easier task.

2. Control Stemming from Factual Influence – This 2nd scenario requires a more thorough and deeper analysis of the equation between the various parties involved within the personal data processing as certain involved parties can exercise control due to business variables such as essential or non-essential means, service level agreements, business agreements, operational risks and cost bearers in case of risk materialization.

The fourth foundational block, **"Purpose and Means,"** for Data Controllers carries substantial importance as it helps in performing a thorough analysis, particularly in cases where a party among all involved parties is able to exercise control due to factual influence.

The EDPB guidelines express that the controller must be able to determine both the **purpose** and **means** associated with personal data processing to be qualified as a controller. It particularly singles out that purpose determination is not the role of the controller, while in means of processing, the processor may provide inputs, suggestions, or even exercise discretion.

The concept of Essential and non-essential means is an extremely valuable one introduced within the EDPB guidelines, as it helps to dissect the level of influence and limitations of that influence. It is pivotal for DPOs to understand how to apply these concepts to be able to come to the right conclusion about the role of a party as a controller or a processor.

- **Essential means** attributes for determining personal data identifiers, retention periods, data classification, recipients of personal data, jurisdictions in which personal data will be processed, and categories of data subjects whose personal data will be processed.

The EDPB guidelines provide express affirmation that such essential means are the mandate and authority of the data controllers.

- **Non-essential means** attributes to mechanisms such choice of hosting location, encryption algorithms, network pathways, operating systems, etc., may be delegated to the processor if agreed by the controller as well. These matters are agreed upon by the controller and the processor using a Data Processing Agreement.

Data Processors - "A processor is a natural or legal person, public authority, agency or another body, which processes personal data on behalf of the controller".

EDPB emphasizes the two major blocks necessary to qualify as data processors, which are given below:

1. Being a separate entity in relation to the controller.
2. Processing personal data on the controller's behalf.

The following EDPB guidelines are essential to understand the above foundational blocks.

- A separate entity means that the controller decides to delegate all or part of the processing activities to an external organization. Within a group of companies, one company can be a processor to another company acting as controller, as both companies are separate entities. On the other hand, a department within a company cannot be a processor to another department within the same entity.
- The processing must be done on behalf of a controller but otherwise than under its direct authority or control.
- Acting "on behalf of" means serving someone else's interest and recalls the legal concept of "delegation". In the case of data protection law, a processor is called to implement the instructions given by the controller at least with regard to the purpose of the processing and the essential elements of the means. The lawfulness of the processing according to Article 6, and if relevant Article 9, of the Regulation will be derived from the controller's activity and the processor must not process the data otherwise than according to the controller's instructions. Even so, as described above, the controller's instructions may still leave a certain degree of discretion about how to best serve the controller's interests, allowing the processor to choose the most suitable technical and organizational means.
- Acting "on behalf of" also means that the processor may not carry out processing for its own purpose(s).

Joint controller is another term expressed under Article 26 of the EU – GDPR.

Joint Controllers - EU GDPR expresses joint controllers as parties "where two or more controllers jointly determine the purposes and means of processing, they shall be joint controllers."

In broad terms, joint controllership exists with regard to a specific processing activity when different parties jointly determine the purpose and means of this processing activity.

Compliance & Operational Costs for Data Processors

Once the two parties agree on a working arrangement regarding personal data processing, then their roles are captured within the data processing agreement, where the role of each party is determined as a controller or a processor.

Before we begin to delve into the discussion of influence and power asymmetry that exists between the data controllers and the data processors, the following section unpacks what adherence to the instructions issued by the data controllers means to data processors and how it culminates in the compliance and the operational costs with a monetary impact on the data processors.

1. **Technical and Organizational Safeguards**

   o Implementation of data security mechanisms such as encryption, pseudonymization, and anonymization.

   o Regular and periodic security testing, such as red team assessment, penetration testing, and vulnerability assessments.

   o Implementation of user access management, SIEM, and Database Activity Monitoring solutions.

2. **Record-Keeping and Audit Support**

Maintaining detailed logs and records of processing activities of categories of personal data processed, their purposes, and sub-processors if they are involved in processing.

Controllers often exercise their right to audit the data processors, subject to which the processors are expected to mitigate the risk associated with the audit observations within a given timeframe. Failing to do so may result in termination of the contract exercised by the data controller.

3. **Data Subject Request Assistance**

In cases where data processors collect, store, and process personal data, they are expected to assist the data controllers in the exercise of the data subject rights. This means that the data processors are expected to allocate technological and human resources to facilitate controllers in serving the requests of the data subjects.

4. **Incident Response and Breach Notification**

Most privacy laws and regulations compel the data controllers to notify data subjects and the supervisory authorities without any undue delay or within 72 72-hour window, respectively. The controllers ensure that such clauses are covered within the Data processing agreement, ensuring that processors are obligated to notify the data controller in case of a personal data breach.

This element entails a cost where the processor must have the organizational and technical means to detect, identify, and qualify that a breach has occurred and there is a need to report such a breach to the controller. The data processors must also have allocated human resources and secure communications channels to carry out these tasks in a timely manner. In cases where the data processor fails to deliver on its commitments expressed within the DPA, it is likely to evoke a penalty or a liability upon the processor as defined within the DPA.

5. Contract Negotiation and Insurance

Since the data processors generally provide services to various clients related to the personal data processing, they prefer securing adequate cyber insurance that can help them to offset the costs they may incur due to the materialization of the risks.

Additionally, the data processing agreements require significant negotiation and mental effort to ensure that the DPAs do not become the source of risk themselves. The data processors often rely on legal counsel to ensure that the processors' interests are well guarded within the DPAs.

The above section highlighted how compliance and operational compulsions can lead to monetary and material cost on the data processors which brings us to a critical point about the dangers associated with the misidentification of the roles between the two organizations particularly the DPOs who are expected to architect the DPA by performing a thorough and deeper inspection of the business arrangements between the two parties.

1. False allocation of responsibility and accountabilities – When a party is misjudged to be a controller or processor due to inappropriate analysis of a business arrangement, then either or both of the parties are expected to suffer due to the erroneous allocation of compliance responsibility.

2. Increase in Cost of Operations – It is more likely to occur when a party is erroneously identified and agreed upon as the data processor, which means that the organization will have to bear the cost of compliance and operations mentioned in the previous section.

- **Example:** Dual Privacy breach-notification channels and redundant privacy impact assessments inflate both time and monetary costs.

3. Data Subjects Become a Casualty – When parties involved in personal data processing are not correctly identified and the responsibilities and accountabilities are not correctly determined, then it leads to a situation where data subjects are left to languish between the parties demanding to exercise their rights enshrined within the privacy laws or regulations.

When DPOs fail to exercise and demonstrate due diligence in identification of controller or processors and later in negotiating and crafting the DPAs with the involved stakeholders, they essentially become the architect of latent chaos which an organization may not be able to discover unless an apocalypse occurs in the form of private right of action by the data subjects, penalties imposed by the regulators or supervisory authorities or the lawsuit filed by the other party.

Power Asymmetry Between Data Controllers and Processors

The conclusions that can be drawn from the previous sections of this chapter are as follows:

- Apparently, Data Controllers wield more contractual power when compared to data processors as they determine the purpose of processing, personal data elements to be processed, lawful purpose of processing, essential means of processing, and take part in identifying the non-essential means of processing.
- Data controllers remain ultimately responsible for the entire personal data processing activity carried out end-to-end. Even though the data processors are independently accountable for adhering to various obligations under GDPR and other privacy laws but their accountability rests in front of the regulators that have granted them the license to offer their services, whereas the data subjects will always look to the data controllers for protection of their data and not to the processors.
- Data Processors are obligated to remain within the boundaries of instructions laid out by the data controllers for personal data processing.
- Data processors are processing personal data only on behalf of or for the benefit of the data controller, with no inherent benefit associated with personal data processing to the data processor.
- Data Processors must bear compliance and operational costs for processing personal data for the benefit of or on behalf of the data controller.

The above points paint a picture depicting that the power equation is tilted towards data controllers. Therefore it's incumbent for DPOs and privacy professionals to think about the following questions.

Q1. *If power equilibrium is deemed to be in favor of data controllers, then what benefits do the data processors have in this equation?*

Q2. *What benefit do data processors have to be in such an equation where they must bear the compliance and operational cost and remain apparently vulnerable in front of the data controllers?*

Q3. *What is the data processors' business model to optimize such compliance and operational costs?*

Let us begin to unpack these questions and find their answers.

To get to the answers associated with the above questions, it is important to revert to the definition of a data processor as the party that processes personal data only for the benefit of or on behalf of the data controller.

This means that the services provided by the party deemed a data processor are not interested in personal data processing. The party is rather providing the ecosystem, the platform, or the infrastructure without which the data controller won't be able to reap benefits related to personal data processing.

Such dependencies may occur in the form of requiring IT data centers capable of hosting data, providing infrastructure and services such as call centers, easy touch points with data subjects available to processors, etc.

The Data controllers may find it extremely prohibitive in monetary terms and other resources to establish such capabilities necessary to benefit from personal data processing. This means that the data controllers may be significantly dependent on the data processors' capabilities and competencies. This dependency on the data processor helps to debunk perceptions of asymmetry in favor of data controllers.

We will resort to answering question number 3 first, and that will help in providing the answers for question number 2.

The Data processors have accrued competencies and capabilities, whether related to infrastructure, applications, or services that are cost and labor-intensive for an organizational to build. These accrued competencies and capabilities help the data processors to operate at economies of scale, which further helps to reduce the compliance and operational costs. While their costs associated with software development, platform security, and compliance costs may remain in control but as their customers base increase, their overall cost of operations is reduced.

Additionally, their standardized and automated processes further aid in the reduction of the cost as this expertise is multiplied and scaled, which helps to attract newer clients in multiple jurisdictions.

By adopting the above approach, the data processors are able to carve out a business model where the cost of adhering to controllers' requirements is negligible compared to the benefits associated with providing the associated services.

It also shifts the equilibrium in favor of the data processors, where if a controller is adamant on adding more pressing clauses within the Data processing agreement, and if it yields low benefits in a cost-benefit analysis for the processors, then the processors may ask the controllers to seek services from other data processors.

The above business context and market dynamics are extremely important for the data protection officers and the privacy professionals to understand. Superficial analysis always tends to present data controllers as authoritative parties. However, the market dynamics enable the processors to often dictate terms and limit the negotiating power and audit scope of the controllers.

Unpacking Scenarios to Determine Controllers & Processors:

This section is meant to highlight the intricacies of personal data processing between the different parties through examination of the business scenarios.

1. **Bank Processing Payroll Information**

Scenario - Trusted Networks Corporation has taken a service from Atlas Global Bank to process the payroll information of its employees. The Human Resources department uploads the data file every month that contains employees' names, phone numbers, IBANs, and the salary to be credited to the bank account.

Elissa is an employee of the Trusted Networks Corporation, as she joined the organization 2 years ago. However, she has had a current account at the Atlas Global Bank for 8 years.

Both companies want to sign a DPA to mark out the responsibilities and accountabilities of each party.

Examination: In this scenario, Trusted Networks Corporation is working to fulfill its contractual obligations with the employees to dispense their salaries and determines essential means of processing by leveraging the services of the bank. Therefore, they are independent controllers.

However, the banks are also operating under various banking laws, regulations, and circulars issued by the central banks. In order for a bank to deliver such services, the bank may also have to collect and process the personal data for its own independent benefit, which will culminate in purpose determination. The bank is also expected to determine the essential and non-essential means of processing without involving Trusted Networks Corporation in such operational arrangements. This makes the banks independent controllers as well.

It's important to note that many of the organizational employees may already have a customer relationship with the same bank as is the case with Elissa, mentioned above, who opened her bank account 8 years ago.

If the banks begin to accept their position as processors in such business equations, then it will significantly rupture their business because all the organizations seeking such payroll services from the bank will begin to exercise their control and tighten the noose through compliance obligations, which will be counter-productive for the banks and will begin to escalate their operational costs. In crucial circumstances like the occurrence of a personal data breach, the bank will be in a tripartite battle struggling to decide whether to inform data subjects, the central bank, or the commercial clients first or at the same time.

Additionally, the banks will be stripped of their power to determine the purpose and means of processing, which may further debilitate them in fulfilling their compliance obligations put forward by the central banks.

This solution demands a controller-controller relationship between the Trusted Networks Corporation and the bank.

2. Financial Institutions Providing Risk Rating Services.

Scenario - VantagePoint Financial Group (VPFG) offers credit risk ratings for individuals. The group has established a rich database of 200 financial variables that help to identify the financial health and stability of the individuals. The VantagePoint Financial Group has a large client base that benefits from such data to make credit lending decisions.

Crescent Bay Bank recently subscribed to the services offered by VantagePoint Financial Group. In order to fetch a 200 financial variables report, the Crescent Bay Bank needs to input a minimum of 10 personal data elements that are essential to output a report of 200 financial variables.

Crescent Bay Bank intends to sign the DPA, considering itself as the controller while Vantagepoint financial group is a processor. The DPOs at the bank profess that the bank provides the data to the VPFG, which ends up in the database to fetch a report.

Examination:

The first thing that must be examined is whether the VantagePoint Financial Group is designated, authorized, or licensed by the regulatory authority to build a database of 200 financial variables.

If there is no explicit designation or authority granted by the regulatory authority, then we must examine the factual influence. In the above scenario, the 10 data elements submitted by the bank are essentially raw data without any valuable information within them. The bank relies on the valuable information obtained from the VantagePoint Financial Group to determine if an individual is a good candidate to be granted the loan.

The VantagePoint Financial Group is not processing personal data for the benefit of or on behalf of the bank. It is in fact has established such a database of financial variables for pursuing its own commercial interests, the logic, functionality, and lawful purpose of processing are all determined by the VPFG. The data being provided by the bank has no material value to the VPFG. However, the value of the information provided to the bank is more significant, and if the bank does not have such information, it may give birth to credit risk. Additionally, the VantagePoint Financial Group determines the means of processing, including the essential and the non-essential means.

These factors help in determining that both parties are independent controllers who work to process the personal data in their own independent material benefits. The two parties can sign a Controller-to-Controller data processing agreement to honor this personal data processing activity.

3. Medical Insurance services.

Scenario - Trusted Networks Corporation is obligated to provide medical insurance to all its employees. Therefore, the organization obtains the services from Prime Well Health Insurance Company to provide medical insurance to the employees.

Both companies want to sign a DPA to mark out the responsibilities and accountabilities of each party.

Examination – Most of the countries have regulations to regulate the medical insurance services. Therefore, such organizations are obligated to collect and process such personal data for their own benefit. The personal data provided to ensure the employees with medical services is not merely for the benefit of the Trusted Networks Corporation; such data is being used for the benefit of the medical insurance provider as well.

If the medical insurance provider erroneously agrees to become the processor of the trusted network corporation, then it will have to restrict their scope of processing to the instructions issued by organizations that provided such data to the medical service provider. This will be counterproductive for the medical insurance service provider from a business, compliance, and operational standpoint.

Both parties reap benefits from their purpose of processing, which is independently determined. The medical insurance provider independently determines the essential and non-essential means of processing, and therefore it requires a controller-to-controller-based data processing agreement.

4. Cloud Infrastructure services.

Scenario – Zenith Care Hospital has a large chain of branches within the country. They've developed an in-house software application for managing the electronic health records containing clinical data, patient medications, laboratory test results, etc.

The hospital is interested in hosting the application of the famous cloud service provider, which is compliant with the local privacy regulations. The hospital procures infrastructure as a service from the cloud service provider.

Examination – In this scenario, the hospital determines the purpose of processing and has determined essential means of processing by choosing to purchase Infrastructure as a service from the cloud service provider. The hospital may decide upon the data retention periods for the information being stored.

The cloud service provider may choose to implement some non-essential means of processing after due consultation with the hospital, which will be agreed and expressed within the data processing agreement.

The cloud service provider is independent of the hospital and carries no intrinsic benefit from processing personal data, and its interest lies in processing the personal data only on behalf of the processor.

If the hospital chooses to host another software application on the same cloud infrastructure that does not process any personal data, then it would not cause any disadvantage to the cloud service provider.

This requires a controller-processor DPA where the hospital is a controller while the cloud service provider is a processor.

Conclusion

Determining and negotiating your organizational role, either as a controller or processor, requires a thorough analysis and examination of variables between the parties. The European Data Protection Board guidelines provide a valuable and functional understanding to distinguish between controllers and processors.

The EDPB's Guidelines 07/2020 provide invaluable guidance to the DPOs and the privacy professionals to identify and align roles, contracts, and controls to optimize both compliance and operational efficiency.

SOURCES AND REFERENCES

- Narayanan, A. et al., *"Dark Patterns: Past, Present, and Future,"* Communications of the ACM 63(9): 42-47 (2020).

- California Privacy Rights Act, Cal. Civ. Code §1798.140(l) (definition of "dark patterns"); CPRA Regs §7004 (prohibiting manipulative choice architecture)

- FTC Staff Report, *"Bringing Dark Patterns to Light,"* Federal Trade Commission (Sept. 2022) - definition of dark patterns and examples of privacy-intrusive interface designs

- EDPB, *Guidelines 3/2022 on Dark Patterns in Social Media Platform Interfaces* (adopted Mar. 2022) - definition and categories of dark patterns under GDPR.

- Taylor Wessing, *"The DSA: advertising, dark patterns and recommender systems,"* explaining DSA Article 25's ban on dark patterns.

- Epic Games (Fortnite) FTC Complaint (2022) - allegations of dark patterns causing unauthorised charges.

- Central Consumer Protection Authority (India), *Guidelines for Prevention and Regulation of Dark Patterns 2023* - classification of 13 dark patterns and illustrations.

- JSA Law, *"Digital Personal Data Protection Act, 2023"* Prism (Edition 3, 2024) - notes on consent obtained through dark patterns not being valid (drawing from global laws).

- CEUR Workshop (CHI'24) paper on regulatory guidelines - overview of global regulatory efforts (EDPB, FTC, KFTC, India CCPA).

- Irish Examiner, *"Fake countdown timers and constant nagging: The dark patterns…"* (Feb. 2023) - consumer perspective and EU sweep findings.

- https://iai.tv/articles/privacy-the-dark-side-of-control-auid-882

- https://plato.stanford.edu/entries/persons-means/

www.ingramcontent.com/pod-product-compliance
Lightning Source LLC
Chambersburg PA
CBHW041209220326
41597CB00030BA/5133